REAL SELF DEFENSE FOR WOMEN

Written By
ALLEN WOODMAN

Forward by Teri Baldino
(Founder of Ladies Surviving Abuse Foundation)

REAL SELF DEFENSE FOR WOMEN

REAL SELF DEFENSE FOR WOMEN - Written by Allen Woodman is published by Allen Woodman and ARTS EAST PUBLISHING HOUSE releases.

All written, Photographed and/or illustrated material, in whole or in part herein is the sole property of ARTS EAST PUBLISHING HOUSE and Allen Woodman.

Photography by Angie Linton

All rights reserved under the International and Pan American Copyright Conventions.

Distribution of this text and material herein, including but not limited to text, photographs and /or illustrations by photoplay or copy in whole or in part without prior written consent of ARTS EAST PUBLISHING HOUSE or Allen Woodman is strictly forbidden and prohibited by international law.

The publisher of this book is not responsible in any manor whatsoever for any injury which may occur by reading and or following the instructions herein. It is essential that before following any of the activities, physical or otherwise, herein described, the reader or readers should first consult his or her physician for advice on whether or not the activities found herein should be pursued. Since the physical activities described herein may be too sophisticated in nature, it is essential that a physician be consulted.

© REAL SELF DEFENSE FOR WOMEN BY ALLEN WOODMAN

Allen Woodman / Arts East Publishing House

REAL SELF DEFENSE FOR WOMEN

1st printing Copyright – 2019   Printed in USA 2019.

DEDICATION

To all the women in my life who have shown me their strength and resilience. No matter what the odds you can accomplish anything.

A Special thank you to Angie Linton for her invaluable support and all the photography that went in to the making of this book.

Much Love

REAL SELF DEFENSE FOR WOMEN

FORWARD By Teri Baldino (Ladies Surviving Abuse) Page 7

Introduction to Safety   Page 19

CHAPTER 1   What's in a Number?   Page 41

CHAPTER 2   A place you may not want to be   Page 63

> Myth Vs. Fact   Page 64

CHAPTER 3   Where in the World?   Page 77

> Ethiopia   Page 81
> Shri Lanka   Page 83
> Canada   Page 86
> France   Page 88
> Germany   Page 90
> United Kingdom   Page 92
> India   Page 94
> Sweden   Page 96
> South Africa   Page 98
> United States of America   Page 102

CHAPTER 4   How Do You Feel Now?   Page 104

TABLE OF CONTENTS

CHAPTER 5	What's In Your Wallet?	Page 115
CHAPTER 6	What's New?	Page 137
CHAPTER 7	Resistance Tactics	Page 156
CHAPTER 8	Real Self Defense Techniques	Page 167

- ➢ Rear Choke Grab Defense — Page 170
- ➢ Front Single Hand Attack / Grab Defense — Page 199
- ➢ Front Double Hand Attack / Grab Defense — Page 214
- ➢ Front Attack / Grab Daily Item Defense — Page 228

CHAPTER 9	Call For Help	Page 250
ABOUT THE AUTHOR		Page 275
Accompanied Self Defense Contributor		Page 281
Contributors		Page 284
About C.R.I. Counter Terrorism Training School		Page 285
Sources		Page 288

An American is sexually assaulted

An estimated **68%** *of victims* **NEVER REPORT THEIR ASSAULT**

BY TERI BALDINO

FOUNDER OF LADIES SURVIVING ABUSE

I am Teri Baldino, and the one thing I have learned in life is that your life can change in a split second.

I was a pretty happy go lucky teenager at 17. I was not a wild party type girl. I did what most average teenage girls did at that time. One time. I was diligently working on becoming a model - schooling, training, diet and all that wonderful hard work. I often dreamed of being a glamorous model. Posing in amazing clothes and upscale fashion for others to admire.

Just before my eighteenth birthday. I was going out on a date with a guy I met through a friend. This is my third time dating anyone. But this was the first time with this guy. I was turning 18 the next day but little did I know that night would change my life forever.

We were at a house party, walking through the various rooms in the house smiling and talking briefly to friends and acquaintances. The music played in the background and drowned out the sounds of distinct conversations. As we made our way around the large house. We walked into another room and started kissing. He closed the door.

The next thing I knew I was trying to fight him off of me. As he ripped my clothes off and was holding me down, I was screaming, kicking and trying with all my might to stop him. The music was very loud, there were a lot of people laughing and dancing, but no one heard me. He totally overpowered me.

After he finished having his way with me, he simply got up and left the room. Seemingly not interested in me any further and with no remorse of his actions seconds prior.

I went home with a coat over me and never spoke a word to anyone, feeling that my father would somehow blame me for my date's actions. The reasons for this was I was raised in a strict Catholic upbringing with both parents very involved in the church and community. Now I went from that happy go lucky teenager to an ashamed and broken person, feeling dirty, ugly and shamed. I too felt it was my fault.

After turning 18, afraid my parents would somehow find out my dark untold secret, I left home I later met a man ten years older than me. We dated and I thought he was the love of my life. We soon moved in together not knowing that he would be the monster that almost took my life.

The next year and a half would be a living nightmare.

Did I see red flags? No! Did I know a person could be so evil? No!

I was raised with the thought that all people were good. I felt sorry for sad people, for lonely people and for angry people. I had been raised to be kind to everyone, love one another and always turn the other cheek. I was young, what did I know at the time?

Within days after I moved in with him, I found myself beaten, restrained and total overpowered. I was used as a sex object. I was moved far from my home and my family, not allowed to go anywhere, padlocked inside a basement apartment. I felt I was in a prison. One day He left his job and then made it his job to keep me from going anywhere. He had taken my car and destroyed it. No phone, no friends, I was not even allowed to talk to my family.

Approximately 5-6 months later, I realized I was pregnant. I was beaten for food being served cold or not on time. I was abused if I put on any make-up or trimmed my hair. I was hit if the place was not clean enough or if I looked at him in any way he did not like. Mind you now, at this point, I weighed about eighty-something pounds if I were soaking wet.

He eventually took me to see a doctor at a free clinic to find out I was around 6 months pregnant. The beatings only got worse. At times, I was held at gunpoint, restrained, beaten and even shot at. The gun was so close to my head when it went off one evening in another angry fit he had, that I could not hear for weeks out of my right ear.

I was afraid to even move from one room to the next. I was even holding my head down as I was afraid of looking at him in what he called my name through the house to find me. I was choked to the point of blacking out more than once. I was bitten if I did not lay still as he had his way with me sexually. And, of course, I was never allowed to go to the doctor for my injuries, no matter how bad they were.

I was broken and numb. I felt nothing at all anymore. Again, I was allowed to go to the clinic only to find out I was within weeks of giving birth. A few weeks later I gave birth to a healthy baby boy –Something I am still thanking God for. That was the first time in over a year I felt anything. But this actually was love at first site. My heart was now filled with joy. That was soon taken over by fear once again. He took me back to my prison. Within weeks the beatings began again. I was nursing my son when he started on one of his beating rampages. I was shielding my son when he almost hit him in the head. At that very moment, a light came on in my head. I no longer had the option to stay. Now having a purpose and reason to live, I had to protect my son.

He finally got a job and would be gone for about 9 hours. I began planning very carefully how I would get out. I was now the Stepford Wife, doing everything he wanted and more. Now gaining his twisted trust, the padlock that was on the only door to go in or out, was left unlocked so I could go outside and hang diapers to dry. He hated the smell of diapers. I washed them so many times so I could go in and out by myself. He had finally let his guard down and I was able to go to my neighbors to use the phone to call my beloved sister. After three short phone calls, we had a plan.

The next day as he went to work and I went outside to hang the diapers, making sure he did not padlock me in, he drove off. I ran in and gathered everything I could for my baby and myself. My sister came and I ran – never to return again. But it did not end there. I left the abuser, but the abuser did not leave me. For the next four years, I moved on average every 5-6 months from one state to another. I was stalked and called the police many times for broken windshields, flat tires and screaming threats. I finally got what they called at that time, a peace bond against him (now called a restraining order). It did little to no good. The only good part was that the police finally believed me. When he (the abuser) did his dirty work, it would be late at night when I was alone. The magic hours were usually 2, 3 or 4 am. He would hit and run. All I could do was show the police the aftermath. When I moved to another state, I very quickly found out that the peace bond did not follow me. It was not valid in any other state.

The very last and final time that he came after me (mind you four years now), he was going to try and make this the last day of my life. I worked until 3 am and was asleep on my couch in the living room. I always slept with a knife under my pillow. I thank God my son would be sleeping overnight at the babysitters. At about 4 am, one of his most famous hours, I was startled awake by a loud noise. It was the front door of my apartment being kicked in. Before I could even begin to comprehend what was happening, I tried to grab for my knife, but it fell between the arm of the couch and the cushion. He rushed in, grabbed me and threw me across the living room.

I was beaten black and blue. I was bloody and my clothes were ripped. I can't tell you how long the beating went on. The landlord who lived upstairs worked the night shift. The man who lived below me was deaf. It was only a 3-story flat, so no one heard anything. As he was beating me, he told me "if I can't have you, no one can. I am taking you to the park down the street where I will shoot you and hide your body where no one will find you for a very long time, if ever".

With the anger and the look in his eyes, a very cold, dark, evil, hollow stare, I knew he meant every word. As he pulled me down the stairs, he told me he had his gun in his car. He told me I was to get into his car and to not do anything, even to try to run away. As he reminded me, he's an excellent shooter. I knew if I got in that car, I would be dead. He loosened his grip on me and in that split second, I turned and ran as fast as I could. I was watching him reach into his car and then took off running between the buildings. At the end of the yard, I began scaling a 6-foot cinder block wall.

The sun was just starting to come up. All I could think of was to get somewhere other people would be. I thought of a restaurant that was open 24 hours just down the block. Running as fast as I could, not stopping or looking back, I finally made it in the front door of that restaurant. As I opened the door, I yelled: "help me please – he's going to kill me". Heads turned, mouths dropped open, I was a bloody mess, ripped clothing, no shoes – no nothing.

A waitress that recognized me took me by the hand and led me to the back booth away from the windows and doors. She got ice and a cloth and started to help stop the bleeding – then called the police. The police came and called an ambulance. I was taken to the hospital. I had broken ribs, broken nose, sprained wrist, and shoulder, black and blue from one end to the other. When I was released from the hospital, I asked the police if they would take me to my home and check the apartment out to look for him. They had me wait as I told them I was too afraid to walk in alone. They checked every room for me and then walked me in, only to find my cat dead and his blood all over.

With the help of friends, I was able to move out of the apartment that day and out of that state. After that, I found a new friend, a German shepherd that helped guard my home. Thanks to God that was the last time I saw him.

Many more years of my life went on and I began to feel more happiness but never stopped looking over my shoulder. As my life went on, I simply tucked everything deep down inside, hoping never to open it back up again. Years passed by, my life had finally moved on, but only to find myself raising 4 children as a single parent. Doing this for approximately 9 years, sometimes working two jobs, tired and still broken inside,

I met an old classmate online. We talked for hours exchanging emails, progressing to phone calls. We lived literally thousands of miles apart. We decided to meet in person. I was now in my mid-forties. I wanted happiness and a person to share my life with. Longing for companionship, wanting more for my children, a father figure around more often, better schools – I wanted all of this.

I thought I had met Mr. Wonderful. Once again, did I see red flags? No! By the way, I did not even know most of the red flags. Keeping things shoved down deep inside me and never letting them out kept me blind as to what I now know. We dated long distance for a year and a half. Did I know he was only on his best behavior when we were together – of course not? I thought that was just the way he was.

I was captivated by wonderful love letters, flowers sent often, surprise visits, car doors opened, bags being carried, lovely planned nights out, plane tickets being sent to me to visit him, meeting his children and his parents. Everything seemed familiar – we went to the same schools, grew up in the same neighborhood, even twice in the same classrooms. Thinking I've known him pretty much all my life – he was the first boy I ever kissed. It was on the playground. Who would forget that? Thinking I could surely trust him, I had known him for many years. As time went on, we married, and I agreed to move to the state he lived in. He had a great job, lived in a good town with awesome schools for my children.

The first-year things were not too bad. They slowly got worse, everything becomes my fault. He began to belittle and degrade me. He started picking on my children. I watched him slowly become more and angrier. It then became about money and anything and everything was wrong. Before I even realized it, he had slowly been chipping away at me. I was now a skeleton of what I had become. I didn't give him enough attention, I wasn't there enough for him, of course, now we had three children in the house. It wasn't enough cleaning the house, helping the kids with homework, cooking, sporting events, laundry, fixing up the house, painting the exterior and interior, along with having a full-time job. Nothing was enough.

REAL SELF DEFENSE FOR WOMEN

The financial abuse began – he let me know it was not my house, it was his house. He didn't want to pay money for the kid's snack food. So now we had separate bank accounts. He then began to physically attack my children. By this time, I was such a mess that I was on every medication you could think of – high blood pressure, anti-depressants, anti-anxiety, something for sleeping, along with a glass or two of wine. I could almost sleep through anything.

At this time, my father had passed away and then my baby brother passed on. My sister had cancer. I didn't know what end was up. Our sex had become abusive, demanding and controlling. When anything came up, he wanted to do, I had to be there at his side, wearing the clothes he wanted me to wear. I was told how to dress, how to look and how to act. My daughter couldn't take it anymore. She left home after being physically attacked. After she left, his focus was now to physically attack my son. I got my son out of there. I put my son on a plane and sent him to live with his father.

I had no close friends - all my time was spent with him and the kids. He knew I had no one to really confide in. If I was on the phone when he came home, especially with a family member, he would take the phone away from me and hide it.

Now with the kids out of the house, I was now the main target for all of the abuse. I found out he was having an affair, only later to find out he had many. The physical, emotional, sexual and financial abuse had become more than I could bear.

I started to once again plan. I did not get much of my plan into motion before we had a huge fight. He was chasing me around the house – shoving me, threatening me. I grabbed the phone to call 911. He yanked the phone plug out of the wall. I grabbed my cell phone and as I was dialing, he got ahold of me and broke three of my fingers and twisted my wrist so bad that I could no longer hold the phone. I ran into the bedroom to grab the other phone to call them again, as it began to ring, the dispatcher was on the other end. I screamed for help and was told to stay on the line and started asking questions. I was shaking so bad I could hardly talk. He was throwing anything he could pick up at me. The dispatcher told me to get out of the house. He tried blocking me from leaving as I gave the dispatcher a blow by blow description. I finally got outside and stood out by the street waiting for the police to show up.

Once a cop questioned me outside while two others were inside talking to him. By the time the police were done, they decided it was more my fault. And at this point it was what they called a "he said, she said". I knew there was nothing more I could say to the police at this point. I called my oldest son to come and get me as he had recently moved to this state. He came and helped me grab some of my belongings and I went to stay with him. I went to the clinic early in the morning. After the x-ray, splints and being cast, the doctor filed a report on her findings and let me take them to the police – which did no good whatsoever.

By now you should know the story. I went through the stalking, both cyber and physical, finding myself looking over my shoulder all over again. I called the police who told me "he is still your husband, so he has every right to know where you are. We can talk to him but until you are divorced, we cannot do anything".

I called an attorney and filed for divorce. It had been more than 30 days since the last physical attack so I could I could not get a restraining order. I went to a woman's center for help, my doctor and anyone I thought could help me. I went through counseling, therapy, and group sessions. What a great eye-opener! I had a wonderful female attorney – she was awesome. I had documented everything I could – police reports, recordings, and all the calls, the stalking, and pictures on my phone – trust me I took pictures of everything. I was on the road to getting better.

Then my awesome attorney suddenly died. The attorney who took over was of little or no help. He advised me to get over it and move on. The mediation went nowhere. After many tries, I finally gave up and let it all go. He basically got everything including my clothes.

I got a beat-up old car, got it to pass smog, took what I could fit in my car and literally drove thousands of miles far, far away. For the next two years, I tried to lay low as I was told he was still looking for me. I worked on myself and did everything I could to gain as much knowledge as possible. What I did learn is there is very little help out there. You have to tough it out through your own recovery.

A little over 3 ½ years ago I wanted to make a change in this world to help other women to get through this horror. I wanted to teach them the red flags I never saw or knew and how to protect themselves from these monsters and predators. The more I grew and met new people, I found myself becoming stronger, had more self-respect, courage, and wisdom. That was when I started my new journey in life. I wanted to help women all over the world. I wanted to be that someone who could understand exactly what they are going through. Someone who could hold their hand and give them the tools and knowledge to help guide them every step of the way. To help them rebuild a safe new life with dignity, self-respect, and self-reliance.

I have no regrets because God was melting and molding to give me the knowledge and understanding for the purpose of my lifelong journey.

Due to my experiences in life, I started a non-profit 501C3 Ladies Surviving Abuse, and so it was born. My thinking was that I was strong enough to fight any man off. But it is not strength, it is training and knowledge. Thank you, God, for with your help I am a SURVIVOR.

Ladies Surviving Abuse strives to provide a new start to a safe, productive, and fulfilling life for survivors of both physical and mental abuse. We want to equip women with the tools, both physical and mental, to move forward to a healthy and safe beginning.

Far too many women leave abusive relationships to find themselves with nothing more than the clothes they wore on their back when they made the brave leap to walk away.

Our mission is to hold the hands of these women, as they step forward into their new lives.

The foundation lends support through donations like

- Food
- Clothing
- Help in search for employment
- Computer access
- Safe phone numbers to be contacted at
- Legal Advice
- Assistance in finding safe housing
- Group meetings
- Counseling

REAL SELF DEFENSE FOR WOMEN

Countless women continue to live in fear day after day due to the fact they know they will be without these basic necessities, should they leave their abuser.

No matter you how you choose to help, whether in financial support, donations, or simply sharing a link to this page, we are incredibly thankful for helping us help the women who need it most.

As a survivor of domestic abuse for many years, I have been blessed with the ability to have compassion and understanding to know what it is to go through this horrible nightmare. After being raped, beaten, degraded, humiliated and financially abused. I wanted to make a difference in this world.

Seeing first hand that there was no real help out there in this world. I understand what I needed to do. This is how Ladies Surviving Abuse came to be.

Training with Allen Woodman has made me believe in myself and what I can do on my own. I have used and implemented several of the techniques that Allen was kind enough to share with me and my group. With the empowerment that he was able to provide I feel safer and more secure about my own personal security now more than ever.

Teri Baldino

Founder – *Ladies Surviving Abuse*

INTRODUCTION

The security and personal / private defense industry are ever-changing and expansive. Our clients increasingly need to train their personnel to a higher standard. Though security officers are usually the first on scene and they are expected to act similar to their police counterparts, they have little to no training in this regard.

C.R.I. has one of the nation's most comprehensive security officer and private protection academies. The Academy builds a strong foundation for first responders and offers multiple certifications for non-instructor courses as well. We understand that security officers and individuals are not law enforcement, so we emphasize hospitality and customer service throughout our Academy, even offering these as separate units of instruction

Our courses teach everything needed to dispatch a capable security officer, a personal bodyguard or a private individual to overcome a threat, either physically or tactically, including advanced tactics that reduce liability for businesses and their clients.

Our mission is to innovate the greater security industry through our leadership in personal and professional security training.

C.R.I. watches for trends and fluctuations in statistics and events to be better prepared to teach in an evaluated and updated manner. Our idea is to be better prepared for future trends before they come and not after they are already mainstream.

Due to the expanding number of critical incidents happening around the world, C.R.I. developed the Urban Warrior Program to better help Women and those that are targeted for assault or attack. C.R.I. uses the Womens self-defense classes to teach and instruct primarily women how to better defend themselves in an aggressive situation. This program of study equips students with the knowledge to be able to learn and ultimately teach simple methods of defensive tactics, as well as providing them with the tools necessary to be able to leave CRI Counter

Terrorism Training School and start his/her own path of self-reliance and self-defense.

The instructors for the Counter Terrorism and Urban Warrior Self-defense programs for this program have years of martial arts experience and express a passion to instruct others.

In today's ever-growing society, there are some things that do not improve over time. Violence against women is a crime that is ever reaching and exponential in its growth. Not only here in the United States but around the globe.

When I first began writing this book to show real self-defense techniques, I began my research into the reality of violence against women to get a true subjective look at statistics and the reality of its reach in today's environment.

When I found the most recent F.B.I.'s review of the fervent growth of attacks, violence, rape and attempted rape statistics I was filled with grief and remorse of the numbers I came across. Among the information compiled in this text, I have also included the most informative and reliable sources available to me.

Individually each person is responsible for their own safety and their own well-being. It's a nice thought to believe that a white knight would come to the rescue of any damsel in distress, however, in most cases, this is not the reality and not a method I would recommend to any student or person wanting to learn self-defense measures seek. It is up to each separate individual to be aware of their surroundings and to take responsibility for their own personal safety and defense.

REAL SELF DEFENSE FOR WOMEN

In 2018 the United Nations defines violence against women as "any act of gender-based violence that results in, or is likely to result in, physical, sexual, or mental harm or suffering to women, including threats of such acts, coercion or arbitrary deprivation of liberty, whether occurring in public or in private life."

Intimate partner violence refers to behavior by an intimate partner or ex-partner that causes physical, sexual or psychological harm, including physical aggression, sexual coercion, and psychological abuse and controlling behaviors.

Sexual violence is "any sexual act, attempt to obtain a sexual act, or other act directed against a person's sexuality using coercion, by any person regardless of their relationship to the victim, in any setting. It includes rape, defined as the physically forced or otherwise coerced penetration of the vulva or anus with a penis, other body part or object."

The sheer scope of the problem is partially symptomatic of population-level surveys based on reports from victims providing the most accurate estimates of the prevalence of intimate partner violence and sexual violence. A 2013 analysis conduct by WHO with the London School of Hygiene and Tropical Medicine and the South Africa Medical Research Council, used existing data from over 80 countries and found that worldwide, 1 in 3, or 35%, of women have experienced physical and/or sexual violence by an intimate partner or non-partner sexual violence.

Almost one third (30%) of all women who have been in a relationship have experienced physical and/or sexual violence by their intimate partner. The prevalence estimates of intimate partner violence range from 23.2% in high-income countries and

24.6% in the WHO Western Pacific region to 37% in the WHO Eastern Mediterranean region, and 37.7% in the WHO South-East Asia region.

Globally as many as 38% of all murders of women are committed by intimate partners. In addition to intimate partner violence, globally 7% of women report having been sexually assaulted by someone other than a partner, although data for non-partner sexual violence are more limited. Intimate partner and sexual violence are mostly perpetrated by men against women.

A few factors associated with intimate partner and sexual violence occur at individual, family, community and wider society levels. Some are associated with being a perpetrator of violence, some are associated with experiencing violence and some are associated with both.

This data was generated in early 2000 and since then the data has changed. The general information is still a strong understanding of the issue that we all must face currently.

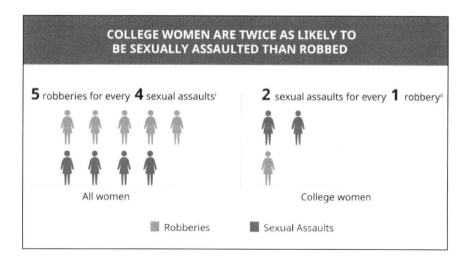

Risk factors for both intimate partner and sexual violence include:

- lower levels of education (perpetration of sexual violence and experience of sexual violence);
- a history of exposure to child maltreatment (perpetration and experience);
- witnessing family violence (perpetration and experience);
- antisocial personality disorder (perpetration);
- harmful use of alcohol (perpetration and experience);
- having multiple partners or suspected by their partners of infidelity (perpetration);
- attitudes that condone violence (perpetration);
- community norms that privilege or ascribe higher status to men and lower status to women; and
- Low levels of women's access to paid employment.

Factors specifically associated with intimate partner violence include:

- past history of violence
- marital discord and dissatisfaction
- difficulties in communicating between partners
- Male controlling behaviors towards their partners.

Factors specifically associated with sexual violence perpetration Include:

- beliefs in family honor and sexual purity
- ideologies of male sexual entitlement
- Weak legal sanctions for sexual violence.

Gender inequality and norms on the acceptability of violence against women are a root cause of violence against women.

Intimate partner (physical, sexual and emotional) and sexual violence cause serious short- and long-term physical, mental, sexual and reproductive health problems for women. They also affect their children, and lead to high social and economic costs for women, their families and societies. Such violence can:

- Have fatal outcomes like homicide or suicide.

- Lead to injuries, with 42% of women who experience intimate partner violence reporting an injury as a consequence of this violence.

- Lead to unintended pregnancies, induced abortions, gynecological problems, and sexually transmitted infections, including HIV. The 2013 analysis found that women who had been physically or sexually abused were 1.5 times more likely to have a sexually transmitted infection and, in some regions, HIV, compared to women who had not experienced partner violence. They are also twice as likely to have an abortion.

- Intimate partner violence in pregnancy also increases the likelihood of miscarriage, stillbirth, pre-term delivery and low birth weight babies. The same 2013 study showed that women who experienced intimate partner violence were 16% more likely to suffer a miscarriage and 41% more likely to have a pre-term birth.

- These forms of violence can lead to depression, post-traumatic stress and other anxiety disorders, sleep difficulties, eating disorders, and suicide attempts. The 2013 analysis found that women who have experienced intimate partner violence were almost twice as likely to experience depression and problem drinking.

- Health effects can also include headaches, back pain, abdominal pain, gastrointestinal disorders, limited mobility and poor overall health.

- Sexual violence, particularly during childhood, can lead to increased smoking, drug and alcohol misuse, and risky sexual behaviors in later life. It is also associated with perpetration of violence (for males) and being a victim of violence (for females).

The initial and morbidly long-term impact on children is also greater than expected.

- Children who grow up in families where there is violence may suffer a range of behavioral and emotional disturbances. These can also be associated with perpetrating or experiencing violence later in life.

- Intimate partner violence has also been associated with higher rates of infant and child mortality and morbidity (through, for example diarrheal disease or malnutrition).

This leads us to the overwhelming social and economic costs due to this violence perpetrated on its victims. Looking at Cost and social analysis it is clear that it undermines our productive growth as a country and its detrimental effects on our citizens.

The social and economic costs of intimate partner and sexual violence are enormous and have ripple effects throughout society. Women may suffer isolation, inability to work, loss of wages, lack of participation in regular activities and limited ability to care for themselves and their children.

There are a growing number of well-designed studies looking at the effectiveness of prevention and response programs. More resources are needed to strengthen the prevention of and response to intimate partner and sexual violence, including primary prevention – stopping it from happening in the first place.

There is some evidence from high-income countries that advocacy and counselling interventions to improve access to services for survivors of intimate partner violence are effective in reducing such violence. Home visitation programs involving health worker outreach by trained nurses also show promise in reducing intimate partner violence. However, these have yet to be assessed for use in resource-poor settings.

In low resource settings, prevention strategies that have been shown to be promising include: those that empower women economically and socially through a combination of microfinance and skills training related to gender equality; that promote communication and relationship skills within couples and communities; that reduce access to, and harmful use of alcohol; transform harmful gender and social norms through community mobilization and group-based participatory education with women and men to generate critical reflections about unequal gender and power relationships.

To achieve lasting change, it is important to enact and enforce legislation and develop and implement policies that promote gender equality by:

- ending discrimination against women in marriage, divorce and custody laws

- ending discrimination in inheritance laws and ownership of assets

- improving women's access to paid employment

- Developing and resourcing national plans and policies to address violence against women.

This complex matter leads us to the initial interest for me to write this book. I wanted to share my personal and professional experience for those seeking help.

The defense of oneself against an aggressor in any given situation that leads to a single outcome of victory over the attacker.

After my years of extensive training in various martial arts and self-defense systems, I had acquired some semblance of understanding of balance, precision and tact and skill. I wanted to share that knowledge with others.

Self Defense is not only physical technique but a mental approach to one's own safety in any given situation. Including but not limited to Physical threats but those also not often realized until it's too late such as, cyber-attacks, bullying and cyberbullying, identity theft and even fraud. These are all subject to a person's direct involvement in their own personal protection.

I have gathered as much helpful information in this text to have a better understanding of the myriad of details and techniques available to make a person feel and become more self-aware of their own ability to protect themselves.

There are several statistics and charts from several leading authorities such as governmental agencies as well as Police and F.B.I statistics and numbers to help define the proliferation of Violence against women.

When reading and viewing the material herein please note that the statistics are as current and up to date as I could resource, but they are not limited to change.

My main objective in this material is to inform and educate the reader about the dangers and violence that plague women in today's society.

While researching for the material that was used in the making of this book I came across facts and figures that I was not ready for nor that I honestly could comprehend. The unfathomable disrespect and actual assault on females simply staggered my own imagination and mystified my mental equity.

I had never given the details of the issue much thought beforehand. I had been teaching martial arts and self-defense classes for women for more than 30 years. I had heard and been referred to certain statistics before but after careful review and mass data input, I was not truly ready for the answers I was set to receive on the topic.

Firstly, let me state emphatically that violence against women is preventable. Violence against women is a result of the unequal distribution of resources and power between men and women and an adherence to inflexible, culturally prescribed gender norms and stereotypes. Violence against women is a set of learned behaviors.

I personally understand that violence against women is a complex social problem with gender inequality at its core. Domestic violence will always exist where there are structural and normative gender inequalities in the fabric of a society. The social work profession uses a 'feminist structural ecological systems analysis' as the core theoretical and conceptual basis for understanding and responding to violence against women. This incorporates an understanding of the complex interplay of gender, ethnicity, ability, race, socio-economic status, sexuality and religion on women's lived experiences of violence.

Violence against women occurs and is perpetrated across all levels of society:

- Institutional and systemic level
- Organizational and community level
- Individual, family and peer group level.

Violence against women is prevalent but preventable. Violence against women has detrimental impacts on women, children, communities, and society, and these impacts have a direct cost at a personal, family, community, societal and economic level. The reduction and eradication of violence against women will benefit society at all of these levels. Not only are there the obvious social, health and moral reasons to reduce violence against women, but there are also significant economic reasons.

The economic and financial toll of violence against women is substantial. Change is required at a structural, attitudinal and service-delivery level across all sections of society. I remain committed to an ongoing professional and personal development in this area in order to ensure that women of all ages, ethnicity, and ages are equipped to defend themselves at all levels to violence in all settings.

In this manual, the reader will find statistics and information related to the aggressive and inclining issue of Violence against women in its many forms. It was not my initial idea to shock the reader with graphic and disturbing data however after many years of research on the subject if it can drive home the importance of knowing real self-defense than I feel I may have educated some.

The truth is that it happens. For what it is worth it happens daily, minute by minute and second by second. As you the reader prevue forward in this material you may learn the horrifying truth of being attacked, its likelihood and its effects both physically and mentally.

These are ever growing issues that seem to be growing in most cases and not decreasing by any means. One should reflect on the numbers and come to the realization that they are not merely numbers. Each number or percentage represents an actual person, mostly women that have suffered unbearable attacks of various degrees not only by strangers but often by persons well known to the victims in many cases.

This is the most disheartening portion of this book. When viewing the resources and numbers listed herein, remember that any one of us is potentially another statistic on the chart and another victim of the problem at hand.

It is up to us to ensure our own safety and self-protection along with self-awareness to our surroundings to not allow ourselves to become another number on a chart or graph.

It is my honest belief that every person should learn a self-defense method or a martial art. With the varied myriad of arts available to the general public, this is a system or school of training accessible to everyone, young or old, male or female.

Training in any system of self-defense can be a health benefit as well as a way to learn to protect one's self against an attack.

In that frame of mind, however, make sure that when you are searching for a self-defense class or Rape prevention course of any kind that you do some due diligence of your own. NOT ALL SELF DEFENSE CLASSES ARE THE SAME OR EQUAL.

Nor are the instructors that teach them! When looking into a class or course ask questions and even go online if possible, to find out more about the school, class, and instructor to see if they meet your standards or what you are looking for.

Many martial arts schools teach some sort of women's protective class but depending on the instructor's background it usually is just a marketing ploy to get you into the school and ultimately sign you up for classes as a regular paying member. They are a business after all and are generally looking after their business interest. Their interest and your interest may diverge and the more you know the better equipped you will be to ask the right questions and know what the right answers are.

HISTORY OF REPORTED DOMESTIC VIOLENCE

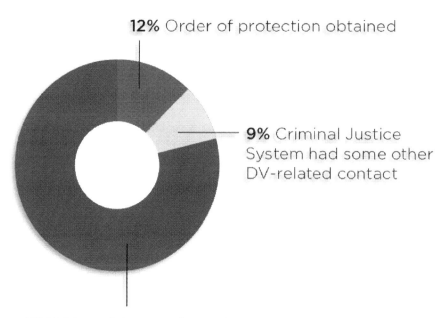

REAL SELF DEFENSE FOR WOMEN

In a published article by Sarah Kliff for VOX.com she reported that there's no universal experience in violence against women; each case is different and unacceptable on its own. There are, however, statistics and trends that show us the state of violence against women in the United States right now.

1. Most women experience physical abuse in their lifetime

The most recent, national survey of American women found that a slight majority (51.9 percent) reported experiencing physical violence at some point in their life. These figures, it's worth pointing out, are from 2000 because that's the last time the Department of Justice released a comprehensive report on the prevalence of violence against women.

This is higher than other developed countries. One-quarter of Swedish women, for example, reported experiencing physical violence during their lifetime. In Italy, the number stands at 18 percent.

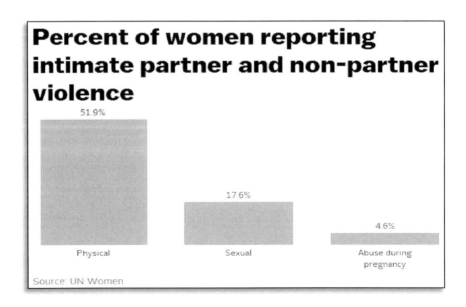

2. Nearly one-quarter of women experience a physical or sexual assault by an intimate partner

About 1.3 million women are victimized annually by an intimate partner, a term which refers to spouses, ex-spouses or significant others.

The rate of violence by an intimate partner is much higher for women than men. One out of five American women report being victimized by an intimate partner compared to one out of 14 American men.

The Justice Department report also looks at rape cases by the relationship to the rapist. The statistics show that the vast majority of rapes (72 percent) are perpetrated by an intimate partner

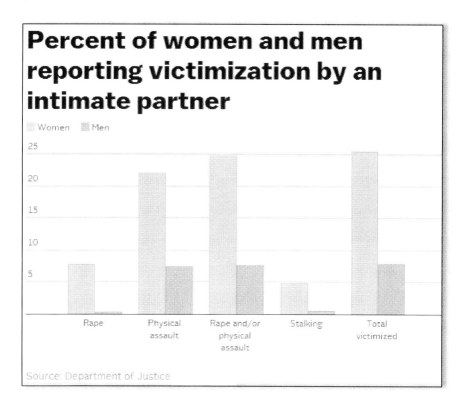

REAL SELF DEFENSE FOR WOMEN

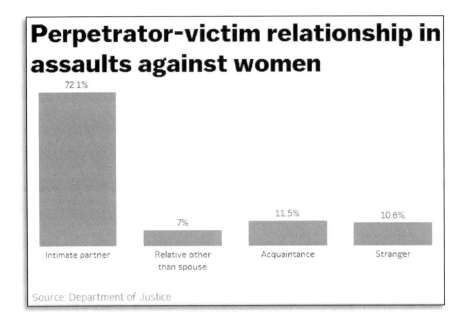

4. One in five women are raped in their lifetime

That's what data collected by the Centers for Disease Control and Prevention show.

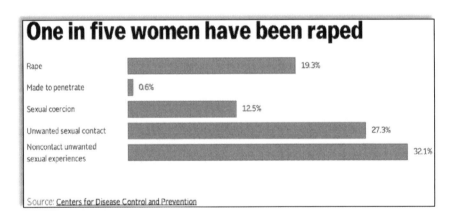

Twice as many women report experiencing some other form of sexual violence, including sexual coercion and other unwanted sexual contact.

The CDC defines sexual coercion as "no physically pressured unwanted penetration," sexual contact as behavior including "kissing or fondling" and non-contact unwanted sexual experience as "being flashed or forced to view sexually explicit media."

5. One in thirteen murder victims are killed by their husband or boyfriend

There were 12,765 murders in the 2012, according the Federal Bureau of Investigations. Of those, 992 were murders of a wife or girlfriend. That works out to about one in thirteen murder victims in the United States being intimate partners of the killer.

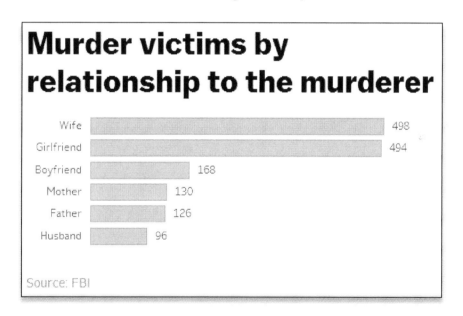

6. One in ten female assault victims has a head or spinal cord injury as a result of the attack

There are other injuries that women report from assault that happen less frequently including chipped or broken teeth, bullet wounds and, in 0.8 percent of physical assaults, women report being knocked unconscious. The variable most likely to predict injury in an assault, the Department of Justice found, was whether the perpetrator threatened to kill or hurt the victim or someone close to them at the time of assault.

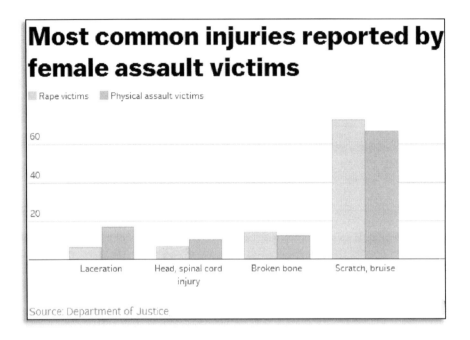

7. But most assault victims don't receive medical care

This is true for both female and male assault victims, although male victims are slightly more likely to receive medical care than females. It's not clear what accounts for the difference, whether male victims are more likely to seek out care, have better access to health services or some other factor is at play.

8. Eighteen percent of mass shooters have a domestic violence charge

Mayors Against Illegal Guns analyzed the 93 shootings that happened between 2009 and 2013, and found that 18 percent of the shooters had previous domestic violence charges. In 57 percent of the mass shootings that Mayors Against Illegal Guns examined, there was a family member (either a spouse, ex-spouse or other relative) who was among the victims in the shooting.

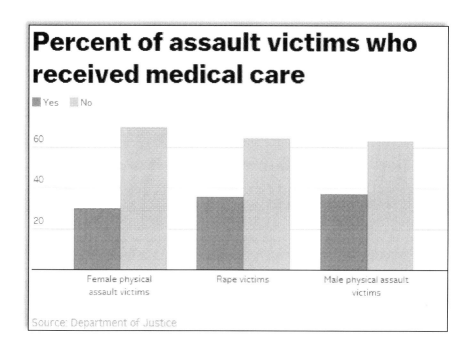

9. Rates of sexual assault are not declining

The last comprehensive survey on violence against women in America happened in 2000, and it's difficult to know everything that has changed between now and then. But there is some evidence that certain types of assaults are becoming less frequent while other forms of assault are on the rise.

REAL SELF DEFENSE FOR WOMEN

Some of the data put forward in this material has been researched and verified by third parties. However, the information and data represented may clash with other corresponding information throughout this manual. The reason that some data may conflict with other known information is due to the time and dissemination of the original research and the specific resource material it was drawn from.

Either way the numbers don't lie, and they are dreadful. The initial concept of this book was to give an honest and up-close view of the staggering war being waged upon women. Violent assault, rape, robbery, humiliation and often homicide are the keys to oppression that women have suffered through for years.

Real self-defense to me is knowledge and the counter-balance of how to use that knowledge to one's own self-interest and self-defense.

Timeline of Crime

- Every 24 min – a murder happens
- Every 4 sec – a theft happens
- Every 5 min – a rape happens
- Every 19 sec – a violent crime happens
- Every 2 ½ min – a sexual assault happens
- Every 29 sec – an assault happens
- Every 54 sec – a robbery happens

CHAPTER 1

WHATS IN A NUMBER?

In the light of the headline issues such as the Bill Cosby scandal, New York Magazine created what may be considered one of the most powerful magazine covers of all time. As in recent articles, stories of rape have stirred serious discussion, thanks in large part to social media.

At the center of this scandal is a simple truth: There are millions of victims of sexual assault worldwide, but social stigma, among other factors, prevents many victims from speaking out and seeking help. A closer look at the numbers surrounding these crimes reveals even more disturbing trends. (And that's not accounting for the fact that most rapes go unreported.)

To shed light on this subject, the Rape, Abuse & Incest National Network (Rainn.org), America's largest anti-sexual violence organization, has compiled numbers from the FBI, Bureau of Statistics, and U.S. Department of Justice to give us a clearer picture of what is happening in the U.S. From the sheer volume of rapes, to convictions, to demographic breakdowns, these are the powerful statistics you need to know.

The simple fact that any amount of rapes or violent sexual assaults are never reported is somehow inconceivable. The victims that have already gone through a horrible ordeal such as rape or a sexual molestation often feel tormented and conflicted about reporting such crimes. Often the victims place blame upon themselves or feel somehow responsible for allowing such actions to have taken. All of these thoughts, however, are not true and anyone that has been involved in such a crime should immediately seek out law enforcement and medical help and support to work through such a tragic event.

The number of victims that know their attacker personally are higher than one would think. This counterbalances the ideas that rape is just something that happens to some people on the street or women that should not be in a certain location.

This should be a wakeup call to victims of rape or sexual assault that even with those you may feel safe with may be the ones you should suspect of acts of violence against you.

As a rule, you should trust yourself with whom you feel safe to be around or with. Your gut is the best instinct if you listen to it.

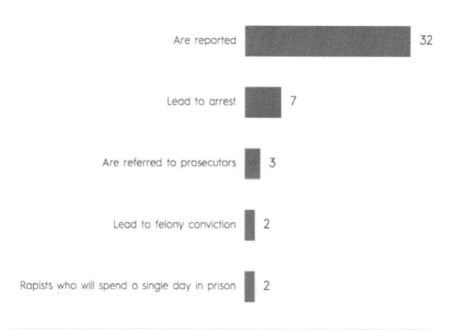

Only 2% of Rapists Serve Time

Even when rapes are reported, few rapists are arrested and convicted. Out of every 100 rapes (including unreported):

- Are reported: 32
- Lead to arrest: 7
- Are referred to prosecutors: 3
- Lead to felony conviction: 2
- Rapists who will spend a single day in prison: 2

REAL SELF DEFENSE FOR WOMEN

There are far too many incidents where people use hindsight to see that they felt uncomfortable with a situation or a person and didn't listen to their own advice or gut feelings.

You should regularly have friends that know where you are and who you are with. An approximate time when you will be back home and even a safety contact that you can call or text to let them know you are safe.

Parents are usually the best for this, but good friends you have known for some time and feel safe with are a great backup as well.

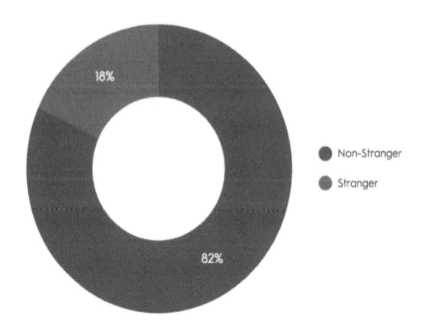

Percentage of Women Who Have Been Victimized, by Race

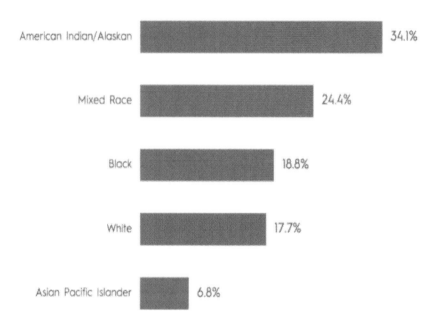

- American Indian/Alaskan — 34.1%
- Mixed Race — 24.4%
- Black — 18.8%
- White — 17.7%
- Asian Pacific Islander — 6.8%

AGE AT WHICH YOU ARE MOST LIKELY TO BE THE VICTIM OF A SEXUAL ASSAULT

MALE: 4
FEMALE: 14.6

SOURCES: RAINN.ORG, U.S. BUREAU OF JUSTICE

THE AVERAGE AGE OF A RAPIST:
31
SOURCE: U.S. DEPARTMENT OF JUSTICE

REAL SELF DEFENSE FOR WOMEN

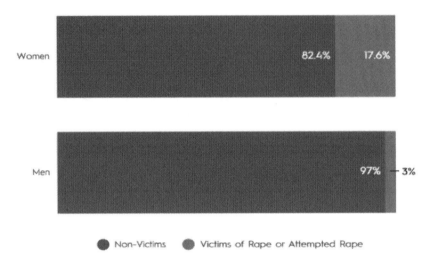

To assume that you are safe today and that you feel you are personally out of range of a would-be attacker and that the circles you run in, that it just doesn't happen, would be an arrogant and disturbing telling of what you do not know.

The assumption that your area or city or region is out of the danger range of such monstrous persons would be in the realm of unfathomable stupidity and below the common sense of a flea. It can happen anywhere and to anyone at any time of the day or night.

Sexual violence encompasses a variety of criminal acts—from sexual threats to unwanted contact to rape. Sexual violence is pervasive and often traumatizing to its victims. For a number of reasons, however, including the stigma and insensitive treatment often associated with these crimes, sexual violence remains highly underreported.

Sexual violence is also a difficult concept to measure, primarily due to inconsistent definitions of sexual assault and rape; differing reporting requirements across local, state, and national law enforcement; and low conviction rates. While people of all genders and gender identities are victims of sexual violence, the majority of these acts are perpetrated by male offenders against female victims. Most victims know the perpetrator in some capacity, either as a friend, acquaintance, family member, or intimate partner.

Over their lifetime, an estimated 19% of women and 2% of men will have been raped, while 44% of women and 23% of men will experience some other form of sexual violence. According to the Bureau of Justice Statistics, in the 10 years from 2006 to 2015, the rates of sexual violence for both women and men experienced no significant change. Rates of sexual violence reported to police also did not change significantly from 2006 to 2015. Consistently across this period, an average of 33% of sexual victimizations were reported to police.

In 2010, 38% of heterosexual female rape victims were 18–24 years old when they were first raped; 28% were first raped between 11 and 17 years old. In 2011, 64% of multiracial women and 40% of multiracial men had experienced some form of sexual violence other than rape. In 2016, an estimated 14,900 military members experienced a sexual assault in the year prior—a decrease from 2014. Of inmates in state and federal prison in 2011–2012, 4% reported experiencing sexual victimization.

In 2015, the Association of American Universities (AAU) published a report on sexual assault and sexual misconduct. Based on a survey of more than 150,000 students at 27 universities, their findings indicated:

- 11.7% of student respondents reported experiencing some form of nonconsensual sexual contact.
- The most common reason for not reporting sexual assault and sexual misconduct victimization was that students did not consider the victimization to be serious enough.
- Other common reasons for not reporting sexual assault and sexual misconduct included the fear that nothing would be done, embarrassment, and emotional distress.

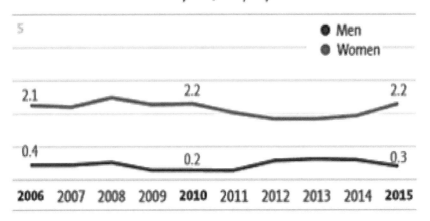

CURRENT DATA ON SEXUAL VIOLENCE

According to the 2010 National Intimate Partner and Sexual Violence Survey (NISVS), **about half (51%) of female victims** of rape reported being raped by an **intimate partner,** and 40.8% by an acquaintance. For **male victims, more than half** (52.4%) reported being raped by an **acquaintance**, and 15.1% by a stranger.[f]

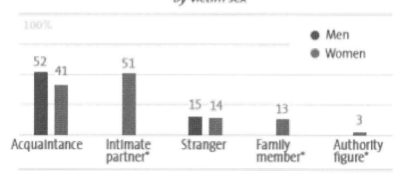

Estimates not reported for men due to small sample size.

It is estimated that 35 percent of women worldwide have experienced either physical and/or sexual intimate partner violence or sexual violence by a non-partner (not including sexual harassment) at some point in their lives. However, some national studies show that up to 70 percent of women have experienced physical and/or sexual violence from an intimate partner in their lifetime. Evidence shows that women who have experienced physical or sexual intimate partner violence report higher rates of depression, having an abortion and acquiring HIV, compared to women who have not.

Similar to data from other regions, in all four countries of a multi-country study from the Middle East and North Africa, men who witnessed their fathers using violence against their mothers, and men who experienced some form of violence at home as children, were significantly more likely to report perpetrating intimate partner violence in their adult relationships. For example, in Lebanon, the likelihood of perpetrating physical violence was more than three times higher among men who had witnessed their fathers beating their mothers during childhood than those who did not.

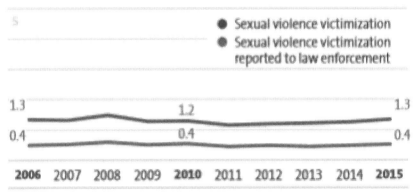

It is estimated that of all women who were the victims of homicide globally in 2012, almost half were killed by intimate partners or family members, compared to less than six percent of men killed in the same year. In Latin America and the Caribbean according to official data from 16 countries, a total of 2,554 women were victims of femicide in 2017.

Adult women account for 51 percent of all human trafficking victims detected globally. Women and girls together account for 71 percent, with girls representing nearly three out of every four child trafficking victims. Nearly three out of every four trafficked women and girls are trafficked for the purpose of sexual exploitation.

It is estimated that there are 650 million women and girls in the world today who were married before age 18. During the past decade, the global rate of child marriage has declined—from one in four young women (aged 20-24) being married as children, to almost one in five. Still, in West and Central Africa—where this harmful practice is most common—over four out of 10 young women were married before their 18th Child marriage often results in early pregnancy and social isolation, interrupts schooling, limits the girl's opportunities and increases her risk of experiencing domestic violence.

At least 200 million women and girls alive today have undergone female genital mutilation in the 30 countries with representative data on prevalence. In most of these countries, most girls were cut before age five. With population movement, female genital mutilation is becoming a practice with global dimensions, among migrant and refugee women and girls.

Approximately 15 million adolescent girls (aged 15 to 19) worldwide have experienced forced sex (forced sexual intercourse or other sexual acts) at some point in their life. Out of these, 9 million adolescent girls were victimized within the past year. In most countries, adolescent girls are most at risk of forced sex by a current/former husband, partner or boyfriend. Based on data from 30 countries, only one percent ever sought professional help.

Globally, one out of three students (aged 11 and 13 to 15 years) have been bullied by their peers at school at least on one day in the past month, with girls and boys equally likely to experience bullying. However, boys are more likely to experience physical bullying than girls, and girls are more likely to experience psychological bullying, particularly being ignored or left out or subject to nasty rumors. Girls also report being made fun of because of how their face or body looks more frequently than boys. School-related gender-based violence is a major obstacle to universal schooling and the right to education for girls.

Twenty-three percent of female undergraduate university students reported having experienced sexual assault or sexual misconduct in a survey across 27 universities in the United States in 2015. Rates of reporting to campus officials, law enforcement or others ranged from five to 28 percent, depending on the specific type of behavior.

One in 10 women in the European Union report having experienced cyber-harassment since the age of 15 (including having received unwanted, offensive sexually explicit emails or SMS messages, or offensive, inappropriate advances on social networking sites). The risk is highest among young women between 18 and 29 years of age.

In a multi-country study from the Middle East and North Africa, between 40 and 60 percent of women said they had ever experienced street-based sexual harassment (mainly sexual comments, stalking/following, or staring/ogling), and 31 percent to 64 percent of men said they had ever carried out such acts. Younger men, men with more education, and men who experienced violence as children were more likely to engage in street sexual harassment.

Results from a national Australian survey show that almost two out of five women (39 percent) aged 15 and older who have been in the workforce in the last five years have experienced sexual harassment in the workplace during that period, compared to one out of four (26 percent) of their male counterparts. Regarding most common perpetrators, in almost 4 out of 5 cases (79 percent) one or more of the perpetrators were male.

Eighty-two percent of women parliamentarians who participated in a study conducted by the Inter-parliamentary Union in 39 countries across 5 regions reported having experienced some form of psychological violence (remarks, gestures and images of a sexist or humiliating sexual nature made against them or threats and/or mobbing) while serving their terms. They cited social media as the main channel through which such psychological violence is perpetrated; nearly half of those surveyed (44 percent) reported having received death, rape, assault or abduction threats towards them or their families. Sixty-five percent had been subjected to sexist remarks, primarily by male colleagues in parliament and from opposing parties as well as their own.

Alarming Domestic Violence Statistics For 2018

In a more recent article written by Leigh Kellner in October 2018 he addressed the elephant in the room so to speak. He reported within the current data collected that Domestic Violence is a major issue in the US and around the world, and many nonprofit organizations work tirelessly to provide critical support and services to victims.

Every year, more than 10 million men and women in the US are subjected to Domestic Violence. Its impact can be felt far and wide:

1. More than 1 in 3 women (35.6%) and more than 1 in 4 men (28.5%) in the U.S. report having experienced rape, physical violence, and/or stalking by an intimate partner in their lifetime.

2. Nearly 20 people per minute are physically abused by an intimate partner in the United States. For one year, this adds up to more than 10 million women and men.

3. Nearly 1 in 4 women and 1 in 7 men have experienced severe physical violence by an intimate partner during their lifetime.

4. Intimate partner violence accounts for 15% of all violent crime.

5. In 15 states, more than 40% of all homicides of women in each state involved intimate partner violence.

6. 85% of domestic violence victims are female, and 15% are male.

7. Women with disabilities have a 40% greater risk of intimate partner violence, especially severe violence, than women without disabilities.

8. 2 in 5 gay or bisexual men will experience intimate partner violence in their lifetimes. Approximately 63% of homeless women have experienced domestic violence in their adult lives.

9. 28% of families were homeless because of domestic violence.

10. Nearly half of all women and men in the US will experience psychological aggression by an intimate partner in their lifetime.

11. Approximately 5 million children are exposed to domestic violence every year. Children exposed are more likely to attempt suicide, abuse drugs and alcohol, run away from home, engage in teenage prostitution, and commit sexual assault crimes.

12. 40% of The Center for Violence-Free Relationships' domestic violence cases have children under 18 in the home.

13. Nationally, 50% of batterers who abuse their intimate partners also abuse their children.

14. Worldwide, men who were exposed to domestic violence as children are 3-4x more likely to perpetrate intimate partner violence as adults

REAL SELF DEFENSE FOR WOMEN

15. 81% of women and 35% of men who experienced rape, stalking, or physical violence by an intimate partner reported significant short- or long-term impact such as post-traumatic stress disorder symptoms and injury.

16. 4% of high school students report being hit, slapped, or physically hurt on purpose by their boyfriend or girlfriend in the last 12 months.

17. Only 1 out of 3 people who are injured during a domestic violence incident will ever receive medical care for their injuries.

18. Most cases of domestic violence are never reported to police.

19. Men who are victimized are substantially less likely than women to report their situation to police.

DOMESTIC VIOLENCE IS ONE OF THE MOST CHRONICALLY UNDERREPORTED CRIMES

25% of all physical assaults committed against females by their partners are reported to the police

20% of all rapes committed against females by their partners are reported to the police

50% of all stalking committed against females by their partners are reported to the police

And for the number of cases that do get reported... a woman will be assaulted by her partner/ex-partner on average **35 TIMES** BEFORE REPORTING IT TO THE POLICE

According to the National Coalition Against Domestic Violence

In June 21, 2018, Advocates joined a congressional panel sponsored by the National Domestic Violence Hotline to examine the state of domestic violence in America today. The panel, led by The Hotline's Chief Executive Officer, Katie Ray-Jones, briefed a packed room of congressional staffers about trends, demographics, and emerging and unmet needs of victims and survivors of domestic violence revealed in the 2017 Impact Report. Representatives from The Hotline, Department of Health and Human Services and Avon discussed insights identified by the data. Senator Bob Casey (D-PA) and Senator John Cornyn (R-TX) attended the briefing and made brief remarks. Both legislators are co-sponsors of the Senate's bipartisan effort to reauthorize funding for the Family Violence Prevention Services Act (S.2784) that provides critical funding for housing and service programs for domestic violence and dating abuse survivors.

One in three women and one in seven men are impacted by domestic violence in their lifetime. The 2017 Impact Report illustrated the many ways in which that abuse plays out in relationships where domestic violence is present, as well as shifts in awareness about abuse for survivors of violence.

For example, between 2016 and 2017, we saw a sharp increase in contacts reaching out for support and referrals related to gun violence. Additionally, we saw a modest increase in contacts reaching out for support related to immigration, however, advocates at The Hotline have noted that many immigrant survivors aren't asking for support outside of protective orders or calling the police due to a heightened fear about detention and deportation. Clearly, there is a need for the supportive services and resources provided by organizations like ours," said Katie Ray-Jones, CEO of The Hotline.

Last year, 323,356 calls, chats, and texts were answered by advocates, but 98,159 calls went unanswered due to a lack of resources.

Senator Casey said, "I am pleased to be working with The National Domestic Violence Hotline, Senator Cornyn, and others to reauthorize the Family Violence Prevention and Services Act. This critically important legislation supports direct services for victims of domestic violence, helping them stay safe as they rebuild their lives. I look forward to continuing to fight for protections and resources for victims of domestic violence."

"These are not partisan issues. These are issues that we try to work together on to help people who need help," said Senator John Cornyn at the event. "The Hotline receives 1,600 calls, texts, and chats each day. It received more than 17,000 last year in Texas alone. These are statistics that demonstrate the dramatic need for the services that have been provided." The 2017 Impact Report by the numbers:

- 74% increase in number of contacts indicating that firearms played a role in their abuse

- 13% increase in number of contacts related to immigration, consistent with a national trend among domestic and sexual violence service providers

- 11% increase in contacts from persons who reported their abusive situation involved children

- 13.7% increase in contacts related to suicide (attempts or threats of suicide used as coercion by abuser)

- Types of domestic violence and dating abuse most discussed in calls (or texts or chats) with The Hotline and Love Is Respect Project, a project of The Hotline that helps educate young people about healthy relationships and dating violence:

- Emotional Abuse: 86% reported some type of emotional and verbal abuse. Emotionally abusive partners often exert power and control over their partners by limiting who their partners see, what they do, and where they go. They instill shame and fear and often demean their partners with insults, threats, and punishments that slowly eat away at their partner's self-worth. Emotional abusers may prevent their partners from making decisions, and sometimes they prevent them from working outside of the home or seeing family and friends – isolating them. We often hear from women that this type of abusive behavior takes place over years before turning physical.

- Financial Abuse: 22% reported their abusers were stealing money or limiting access to money, using their partner's credit cards or forcing their partners to co-sign on lines of credit. Some forced their partners to open joint accounts and preventing them from opening separate accounts or having access to their own money.

- Physical Abuse: 60% reported some type of physical abuse such as hitting, biting, and choking. Physical abuse is often what most people think about when we use the term domestic violence.

- Digital Abuse: 12%. Examples of digital abuse include using GPS or a phone to stalk their partners or track their travel, sending relentless text messaging, closely monitoring computer use and using cameras in the home to monitor activities. The digital abuse category adapts as innovations in technology expand.

- Sexual Abuse: 10%. Abusive partners may do things such as forcing unwanted sexual activity, involving other people in sexual activities without permission, forced viewing of pornography or demanding their partner wear sexually explicit clothing.

Women in the U.S. are more likely to be killed by an intimate partner than by anyone else.

55% of homicides of women involved domestic violence.

93% of these were killed by current or former boyfriends, husbands and partners.

3 women per day are killed by an intimate partner.

The Numbers are truly staggering when looking at them all. There are variations of data and subject to the State, Country, Origin, Date and or year it was collected or Service collecting and disseminating the data can and does fluctuate.

Even if the number were one in a million, I honestly believe that the number would still be too high.

REAL SELF DEFENSE FOR WOMEN

In the course of all this data collection and disbursement I can only reflect that I have a daughter, a Mother, Sisters and personal friends that make this information more hard hitting to me personally. That any woman is often targeted and assaulted in any number is an affront to my own personal moral values and beliefs. It is, however, something that can be changed.

It is not something that America has an issue with only. It is not because of America's loose society or any theories of a corrupt political or legal system. It is a world ide trend that only sees an increase year after year unchanging whether a republican sit in office or a democrat. It seems that violent assaults against women is bipartisan and under enforced globally.

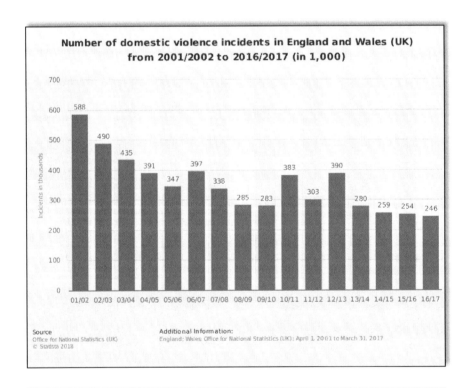

CHAPTER 2

A PLACE YOU MAY NOT WANT TO BE

REAL SELF DEFENSE FOR WOMEN

If we look at the Myths associated with Violence against women and the urban rumors that are combined with those misrepresentations, we can clearly see the need for fact checking to dispel those who would believe in the wrong theories of why and where women are attacked.

MYTH: Victims cause the violence that has happened to them.

FACT: It doesn't matter what someone is wearing or how they are acting, no one asks to be raped. People who sexually assault often use force, threat, or injury. An absence of injuries does not indicate the victim consented.

MYTH: There is no reason for a victim not to report being raped to law enforcement.

FACT: Rape is the least reported and convicted violence crime in the U.S. There are many reasons why victims may choose not to report to law enforcement or tell anyone about what happened to him/her. Some include:

- concern for not being believed
- fear of the attackers getting back at him/her
- embarrassment or shame
- fear of being blamed
- pressure from others not to tell
- distrust of law enforcement
- belief that there is not enough evidence
- desire to protect the attacker

MYTH: Victims provoke sexual assaults when they dress provocatively or act in a promiscuous manner.

FACT: Rape and sexual assault are crimes of violence and control that stem from a person's determination to exercise power over another. Forcing someone to engage in non-consensual sexual activity is sexual assault, regardless of the way that person dresses or acts.

MYTH: If a person goes to someone's room, house, or goes to a bar, he/she assumes the risk of sexual assault. If something happens later, he/she can't claim that he/she was raped or sexually assaulted because he/she should have known not to go to those places.

FACT: This "assumption of risk" wrongfully places the responsibility of the offender's actions with the victim. Even if a person went voluntarily to someone's residence or room and consented to engage in some sexual activity, it does not serve as a blanket consent for all sexual activity.

MYTH: It's not sexual assault if it happens after drinking or taking drugs.

FACT: Being under the influence of alcohol or drugs is not an invitation for non-consensual sexual activity. A person under the influence of drugs or alcohol does not cause others to assault him/her; others choose to take advantage of the situation and sexually assault him/her because he/she is in a vulnerable position.

MYTH: Most sexual assaults are committed by strangers. It's not rape if the people involved knew each other.

FACT: Most sexual assaults and rapes are committed by someone the victim knows. Among victims aged 18 to 29, two-thirds had a prior relationship with the offender.

MYTH: Rape can be avoided if people avoid dark alleys or other "dangerous" places where strangers might be hiding or lurking.

FACT: Rape and sexual assault can occur at any time, in many places, to anyone.

MYTH: It's only rape if the victim puts up a fight and resists.

FACT: There are many reasons why a victim of sexual assault would not fight or resist her attacker. She/he may feel that fighting or resisting will make her/his attacker angry, resulting in more severe injury.

MYTH: Sexual assault is often the result of miscommunication or a mistake.

FACT: Sexual assault is a crime, never simply a mistake. It does not occur due to a miscommunication between two people. Sexual assault is any unwanted sexual contact obtained without consent through the use of force, threat of force, intimidation, or coercion.

MYTH: Sexual assault won't happen to me or to anyone I know.

FACT: Men, women and children of all ages, races, religions, and economic classes, and can be and have been, victims of sexual assault. Sexual assault occurs in rural areas, small towns and larger cities. According to the U.S. Department of Justice, a rape or attempted rape occurs every 5 minutes in the United States.

MYTH: Sexual assault is provoked by the victim's actions, behaviors, or by the way they dress.

FACT: Sexual assault is NEVER the victim's fault. Sexual assault is a violent attack on an individual, not a spontaneous crime of sexual passion. For a victim, it is a humiliating and degrading act. No one "asks" for or caused their assailant to commit a crime against them.

MYTH: Most sexual assaults occur between strangers.

FACT: Most sexual assaults are committed by someone the victim knows: a neighbor, friend, acquaintance, co-worker, classmate, spouse, partner or ex-partner. Studies show that approximately 80% of women reporting sexual assaults knew their assailant.

MYTH: Sexual assaults only occur in dark alleys and isolated areas.

FACT: A sexual assault can happen anywhere and at any time. Many assaults occur in places ordinarily thought to be safe, such as homes, cars and offices.

MYTH: Women falsely accuse men of sexual assault or "cry rape."

FACT: Reported sexual assaults are true, with very few exceptions. FBI crime statistics indicate that only 2% of reported rapes are false. This is the same rate of false reporting as other major crime reports.

MYTH: Men cannot be sexually assaulted.

FACT: Men can be, and are, sexually assaulted. In Colorado one in seventeen men are sexually assaulted in their lifetime. Sexual assault of men is thought to be greatly underreported. Any man can be sexually assaulted regardless of size, strength, sexual orientation, or appearance.

MYTH: Most sexual assaults are interracial.

FACT: Almost all sexual assaults occur between members of the same race. Interracial rape is not common, but it does occur.

MYTH: People who commit sexual assaults are mentally ill, abnormal perverts.

FACT: Sexual offenders come from all educational, occupational, racial and cultural backgrounds. They are "ordinary" and "normal" individuals who sexually assault victims to assert power and control over them and inflict violence, humiliation and degradation.

MYTH: Victims who do not fight back have not been sexually assaulted.

FACT: Anytime someone is forced to have sex against their will, they have been sexually assaulted, regardless of whether or not they fought back. There are many reasons why a victim might not physically fight their attacker including shock, fear, threats or the size and strength of the attacker.

MYTH: A rape survivor will be battered, bruised, and hysterical.

FACT: Many rape survivors are not visibly injured. The threat of violence alone is often sufficient cause for a woman to submit to the rapist, to protect herself from physical harm. People react to crisis in different ways. The reaction may range from composure to anxiety, depression, flashbacks, and suicidal feelings.

MYTH: "If you wouldn't have been drinking, you wouldn't have been sexually assaulted."

FACT: Alcohol is a weapon that some perpetrators use to control their victim and render them helpless. As part of their plan, an assailant may encourage the victim to use alcohol, or identify an individual who is already drunk. Alcohol is not a cause of rape; it is only one of many tools that perpetrators use.

MYTH: Serial rapists are uncommon.

FACT: Most every perpetrator is a serial rapist, meaning that they choose to use coercion, violence, threats of force, etc., to assault people on a repeated basis.

MYTH: When women say no, they really mean yes.

FACT: Yes, means yes! When someone says yes, she/he is explicitly giving consent. Silence does not equal consent. It is the responsibility of the person initiating or escalating sexual activity to gain consent at each level. If you are ever unclear about your partner's wishes, ask for clarification. If your partner says no or seems unsure, respect that person and her/his wishes.

MYTH: If a person is aroused, she/he is assaulted, then it is not sexual assault.

FACT: Orgasm does not mean that someone "enjoyed" the sex, or that they wanted it. Orgasm can be a natural biological reaction that someone can't control; it does not mean that forced or coerced sexual activity was consensual and often this is used to silence the survivor.

Helping to dispel these rumors are just one factor in the education of those who do not understand the factors involved in assault or rape.

Statistics on rape and other sexual assaults are commonly available in industrialized countries and are becoming more common throughout the world. Inconsistent definitions of rape, different rates of reporting, recording, prosecution, and conviction for rape create controversial statistical disparities and lead to accusations that many rape statistics are unreliable or misleading. In some jurisdictions, male-female rape is the only form of rape counted in the statistics and countries may or may not criminalize marital rape.

Rape is severely under-reported. In many parts of the world, rape is very rarely reported, due to the extreme social stigma cast on those who have been raped, or the fear of being disowned by their families, or subjected to violence, including honor killings. Furthermore, in countries where adultery or premarital sex are illegal, victims of rape can face prosecution under these laws, if there is not sufficient evidence to prove a rape in the court. Even if they can prove their rape case, evidence during the investigation may surface showing that they were not virgins at the time of the rape, which, if they are unmarried, opens the door for prosecution.

A United Nations statistical report compiled from government sources showed that more than 250,000 cases of rape or attempted rape were recorded by police annually. The reported data covered 65 countries.

In this section we list the top 10 countries with highest rape crime. You would be amazed to read that the most developed countries like U.S., Sweden, France, Canada, UK and Germany are the most immersed ones in this crime

The number of victims that know their attacker personally are higher than one would think. This counterbalances the ideas that rape is just something that happens to some people on the street or women that should not be in a certain location.

The simple fact that any amount of rapes or violent sexual assaults are never reported is somehow inconceivable. The victims that have already gone through a horrible ordeal such as rape or a sexual molestation often feel tormented and conflicted about reporting such crimes. Often the victims place blame upon themselves or feel somehow responsible for allowing such actions to have taken. All these thoughts, however, are not true and anyone that has been involved in such a crime should immediately seek out law enforcement and medical help and support to work through such a tragic event.

The variance on these numbers is staggering when you realize that a victim is more likely to know their attacker personally by a factor of 4 times.

The Majority of Rapes Are Unreported

According to the U.S. Department of Justice National Crime Victimization Survey (2009-2013), there is an average of 293,066 victims (age 12 or older) of rape and sexual assault each year. Unfortunately, the majority of rapes are still unreported.

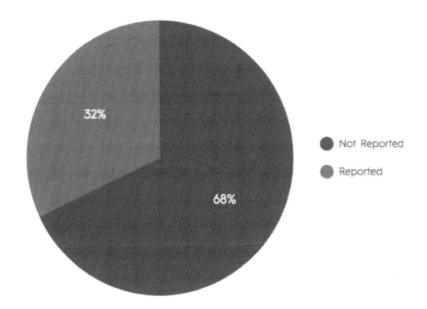

This should be a wakeup call to victims of rape or sexual assault that even with those you may feel safe with may be the ones you should suspect of acts of violence against you.

As a rule, you should trust yourself with whom you feel safe to be around or with. Your gut is the best instinct if you listen to it. There are far too many incidents where people use hindsight to see that they felt uncomfortable with a situation or a person and didn't listen to their own advice or gut feelings.

You should regularly have friends that know where you are and who you are with. An approximate time when you will be back home and even a safety contact that you can call or text to let them know you are safe.

Parents are usually the best for this, but good friends you have known for some time and feel safe with are a great backup as well.

As you read forward into this material it should be noted that most of the current data listed have been developed through the cooperation of the F.B.I. and other Law Enforcement groups. The data can change upon review and update from this publication.

Most Law Enforcement agencies collect and distribute data quarterly and annually and are mostly available to the general public upon request.

These numbers are from the most current F.B.I. Database on rape and violent sexual attacks as of 2017. Any discrepancies of the data collected are unintentional and have been updated since the publication of this material.

Remember that when we speak of statistics and numbers, that they are a conglomeration of data that has been produced and attained through the agencies that have been notified or accounted for an actual attack. The numbers reflect real people that have gone through some of the most horrific and life-altering events that anyone can endure.

The taking of one's personal sexuality in an aggravated way or an assault on one's physical self should never just be a number for the data sheet. These are people with feelings, emotions, families, and lives independent of the attacks or assault that they have endured.

Many must undergo physical, emotional and mental therapy to overcome the brutal attack or rape they have undergone. Some are never able to overcome those scars that are left both physical and emotional.

Authors Dr. Harrison – Senior Lecturer in Law at the University of Hull – and Professor Gill – Criminologist at the University of Roehampton – identified several barriers within British South Asian communities that lead to sexual abuse being even less likely to be reported. These include:

- Honor and consequential shame

    - South Asian culture assigns a higher value to purity than some Western cultures
    - numerous women and girls living in these communities bear the responsibility for the honor of their families
    - if virginity is lost outside of marriage – even through sexual violence – the woman will encounter loss of family honor, along with shame, stigma, public ostracism and, in some cases, forced marriage and honor-based violence
    - once honor is lost, it can never be repaired

REAL SELF DEFENSE FOR WOMEN

- Lack of awareness
    - Low understanding of what constitutes sexual abuse
    - a lack of awareness surrounding marital rape
- Infrastructure
    - Many women were restricted in terms of the buildings they could frequent; this presents a major barrier for those wanting to access services
    - language barriers may also be playing a part
- Modesty
    - As modest and highly private women, even discussing being a victim of sexual violence is seen as dishonorable
- Fear of not being believed
    - As well as fearing that their stories would not be believed, victims fear that ultimately no action will be taken against their abusers leaving them highly vulnerable.

1 in 3 abused
Around the world has been beaten, coerced into sex, or otherwise abused in her lifetime

1 in 20 raped
As well as one in 10 women experiencing some form of sexual violence since the age of 15

2 a week, dead
In the UK, 2 women are killed every week by a current or former male partner

CHAPTER 3

WHERE IN THE WORLD?

The most common misconception of violence against women is the place or location in where it commonly happens. Most common an erroneous thinking is in a seedy motels or dilapidated housing across town. It only happens to women that allow it to happen. The way that a woman dresses or her demeanor in public.

None of these are correct. The sad fact is that it happens far too often and far closer to your home than you would think.

A recent Article posted by Time magazine and written by ELI MEIXLER in November of 2018 stated that The "most dangerous place" for women around the world may be at home. More than half of female murder victims last year were killed by their partners or family members, according to a new United Nations study.

The findings were released by the U.N.'s Office on Drugs and Crime (UNODC) to coincide with the International Day for the Elimination of Violence against Women. The report found that of 87,000 recorded female homicide cases last year, 50,000, or 58%, were committed by the victims' intimate partners or family members. The toll equates to six women killed every hour, or 137 killed every day, by people they know.

"Women continue to pay the highest price as a result of gender inequality, discrimination and negative stereotypes," The UNODC executive director told the press in a public meeting, "The fact that women continue to be affected by this type of violence to a greater degree than men are indicative of an imbalance in power relations between women and men inside the domestic sphere."

The study, part of a forthcoming global report, analyzed homicide data related to gender violence and "femicide," which is defined as a gender-based hate crime. It revealed a stark disparity. While "the majority of intentional homicide victims are male," women comprise the victims of 82% of intimate partner murders. The report also noted that the majority of intimate partner murders corresponded with domestic violence cases.

While Asia recorded the highest total number of female homicides in 2017 with 20,000 cases, the rate of intimate partner or family murder was comparatively low, at 0.9 murders per 100,000 women. By comparison, the highest rates of intimate partner or family murder were found in Africa (3.1 murders per 100,000 women) and the Americas.

The numbers again become staggering when faced with the general fact that these are people that live near you, In your neighborhood, on your block and eerily in your household.

REAL SELF DEFENSE FOR WOMEN

Around the world the numbers do not lie. The rates of rape, murder, violence and abuse are in my opinion way too high.

The malicious attacks and assaults that women must endure in their given lifespan are far too many and far more alarming than one would expect in civilized society.

Nearing 2020, this is something that the entire world needs to address before it becomes too great an issue to resolve. Like that of the tide that cannot be pushed back in to the ocean.

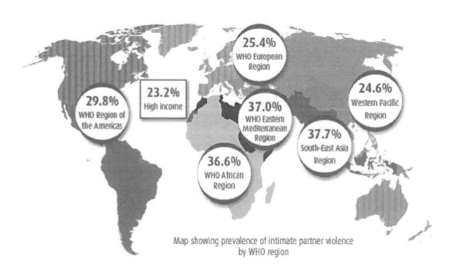

Map showing prevalence of intimate partner violence by WHO region

10. ETHIOPIA

With a large population of well over 100,800,000 people,

Ethiopia is estimated to have one of the highest rates of violence against women in the world. A report by the UN found that nearly 60% of Ethiopian women were subjected to sexual violence. Rape is a very serious problem in Ethiopia.

The country is infamous for the practice of marriage by abduction, with the prevalence of this practice in Ethiopia being one of the highest in the world. In many parts of Ethiopia, it is common for a man, working in coordination with his friends, to kidnap a girl or woman, sometimes using a horse to ease the escape. The abductor will then hide his intended bride and rape her until she becomes pregnant. Girls as young as eleven years old are reported to have been kidnapped for the purpose of marriage.

In no exception, the Ethiopian military has even been widely accused of committing systematic rapes against civilians.

But violence against women remains an entrenched and often taboo issue. Eighty percent of Ethiopians live in rural areas, where patriarchal customs often effectively turn women into second-class citizens.

In cities and towns, Ethiopian and foreign women alike complain of constant sexual harassment on the streets. According to the UN, Ethiopia ranked 121st out of 187 countries in terms of gender equality in 2013.

Using the momentum created by the outrage over incidents of sexual abuse and those resulting in death, activists want to encourage women to speak out against the routine harassment they suffer in the belief it will reduce serious abuse. "If you fail to stop the little things, you're literally encouraging people to do this," was said by a member of the Yellow Movement fighting for women's rights at Addis Ababa University at a rally held at the University in 2016.

There is some uncertainty over the rates of abuse against women in Ethiopia due to inadequate data collection and under-reporting. A 2015 government report said 58-67% of all women had experienced domestic violence. It found that the underlying cause is the low level of status given to women in society coupled with the dominant position of men further justified by culture and religion.

9. SRI LANKA

The current population of Sri Lanka is 20,956,513 as of Friday, August 3, 2018, based on the latest United Nations estimates. Sri Lanka population is equivalent to 0.27% of the total world population.

The UN Multi-country Study on Men and Violence found that 14.5% of the sample of Sri Lankan men had perpetrated rape at some point in their lives. 4.9% had raped in the past year. 2.7% had raped another man. 1.6% had taken part in a gang rape. 96.5% of the men who had raped experienced no legal consequences. 65.8% didn't feel worried or guilty afterward. 64.9% of rapists had raped more than once, and 11.1% had raped four or more girls or women. Sri Lanka has one of the highest suicide rates in the world.

REAL SELF DEFENSE FOR WOMEN

Some observers note the lack of "disaggregated data" concerning violence directed against women as there are no systems in place to collect gender-specific information.

According to a shadow report prepared for the UN Committee against Torture by a collective of Sri Lankan non-governmental organizations (NGOs) dedicated to human rights, it was not found possible to assess the true extent of crimes against women in Sri Lanka because of this lack of open information

Nevertheless, some figures on sexual and domestic violence were found in several sources consulted by the Research Directorate released in early 2009. The UN's IRIN reports that, according to the officer responsible for the Bureau for the Prevention of Abuse of Children and Women of the Sri Lanka Police Department, the police stations nationwide routinely record between 8,000 and 10,000 cases of violence against women per month.

Other sources state that, according to figures recorded by the Police Bureau for the Protection of Women and Children, in 2008, there were 353 reported cases of rape and 963 cases of sexual harassment, while, in 2009, there were 303 reported cases of rape, 841 cases of sexual harassment, and 89 cases of domestic violence as well as 15 cases of "grave sexual abuse".

According to the AHRC report, most women feel that it is better for them not to reveal that they have been victimized.

In correspondence with the Research Directorate, the President of the Institute of Gender and Development Studies of Sri Lanka explained that victims are deterred from taking legal action and procedures that will force them to relive the events without consideration for their privacy and the trauma they have endured.

Sources also report that a victim of sexual violence may suffer a loss of reputation and social standing and have her options for marriage limited.

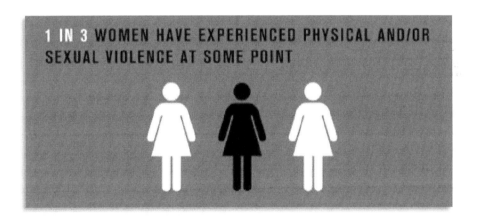

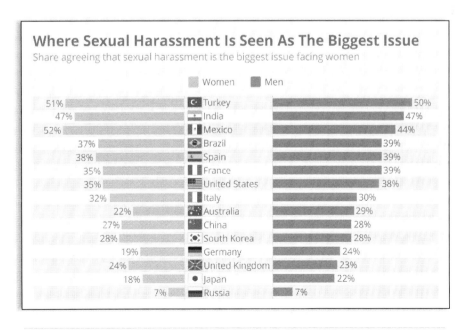

8. CANADA

The current population of Canada is 36,977,464 as of July 29, 2018, based on the latest United Nations estimates. Canada population is equivalent to 0.48% of the total world population.

It is an Amercing continent and the total reported cases of rape in this country are 2,516,918. These are only six percent of the total rape cases. It is reported that over one in three women had experienced a sexual assault and that only 6% of sexual assaults were reported to the police. According to the Justice Institute of British Columbia, one out of every 17 women is raped, 62% of rape victims were physically injured, and 9% were beaten or disfigured.

Statistics Canada says some 3,900 sexual assaults reported to police in 2017 were deemed to be unfounded. In all, 14% of sexual assaults reported to police were given the "unfounded" classification, down from 19% in 2016. The figure is double the

7% of unfounded cases identified among all criminal incidents in Canada last year, Statistics Canada reports this morning in the first reporting of unfounded cases since the agency resumed collecting the data.

Canadian Police give a case the label "unfounded" when officers determine through investigation that the offense did not occur. Sexual assaults are among the least likely crimes to be reported to police, but the last year 28,551 incidents were reported, with the biggest monthly bump seen in October 2017, coinciding with the "#METoo" movement.

Statistics Canada says more severe and violent sexual assaults were less likely to be deemed unfounded than incidents such as unwanted touching or another non-consensual sexual contact. The rate of founded sexual assaults increased by 13% between 2016 and 2017.

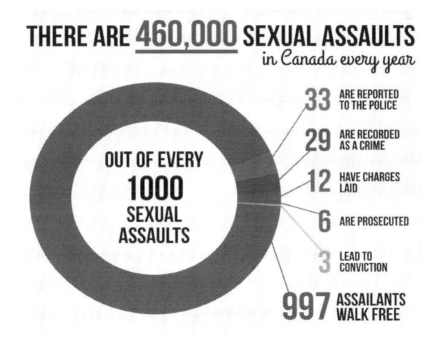

7. FRANCE

The current population of France is 65,254,979 as of August 2, 2018, based on the latest United Nations estimates. France population is equivalent to 0.85% of the total world population.

In a bizarre lack of knowledge, it was highly unknown that rape was not considered a crime in France until 1980. Laws reinforcing women's rights and safety are relatively recent in France. The law-making rape a crime dates back only to 1980. Earlier decrees were based on 19th-century moral codes. A law on sexual-harassment was approved in 1992 and one on moral harassment was passed in 2002. The last bill to fight violence against women was passed last year.

Government studies show there are 75,000 rapes a year in the country. Only about 10 percent of the victims filed complaints. France is at the 7th position with the total reported crime of 3,771,850.

In a recent report by Lucy Pasha-Robinson, it listed over four million women stating that they had been victims of penetrative sexual violence – roughly 12 % of country's female population

Half of the women said they had been verbally insulted or the target of sexist remarks and one in five said they had received pornographic emails or text messages, the report found.

Researchers said they felt compelled to conduct the study to gain a better understanding of the prevalence of sexual misconduct in French society – and measure its effects on victims' health. They believe the problem has become a "major public health issue".

The study also revealed the majority of women surveyed had been affected multiple times and by different types of harassment.

The disturbing figures are revealed amid a global crackdown on the sexual assault and harassment of women and girls.

In France, the "Balance Ton Porc"(rat on your pig) movement has gained widespread traction, with women across the country taking to social media to share their experiences.

44% of victims are under age 18

80% are under age 30

REAL SELF DEFENSE FOR WOMEN

6. GERMANY

The current population of Germany is 82,309,940 as of August 2018, based on the latest United Nations estimates. Germany population is equivalent to 1.08% of the total world population. Germany ranks number 17 in the list of countries (and dependencies) by population.

An estimate of 240,000 women and girls has died in Germany because of this crime. Germany is the number six in the highest rape crime with the figures of 6,507,394 in this year which is really a big figure.

The Federal Criminal Police Office (BKA) together with the German Minister for Family Affairs, Manuela Schwesig, released the statistics in Berlin in 2016. This is the first time the state-run police were releasing numbers showing the extent of violence in intimate relationships, the BKA said in a press statement.

According to the BKA's figures, in 2015, a total of 127,457 people in relationships were targets of murder, bodily harm, rape, sexual assault, threats, and stalking. Eighty-two percent, or over 104,000, of these, were women.

Among the women, over 65,800 suffered simple injuries, 11,400 were badly injured, 16,200 were subjected to threats and nearly 8,000 were victims of stalking. Three hundred thirty-one women were killed intentionally or unintentionally by their partners.

In cases of rape and sexual assault, almost all the victims were women. Over ninety percent of victims of stalking and threats were also female, according to the statistics.

In a press statement, the BKA's President explained that police had registered several cases of abuse, starting from subtle forms of humiliation, insults, and intimidation, psychic, physical and sexual abuse to rape and murder.

EVERY 9 SECONDS

IN THE US,
A WOMAN IS ASSAULTED OR BEATEN

5. UNITED KINGDOM

The current population of the United Kingdom is 66,608,751 as of Saturday, August 4, 2018, based on the latest United Nations estimates. The United Kingdom population is equivalent to 0.87% of the total world population. The U.K. ranks number 21 in the list of countries (and dependencies) by population.

Reportedly one in five women in England and Wales have been subject to sexual assault, official figures show, prompting renewed calls for an injection of funding into support centers for victims.

More than three million women are estimated to have been victims of offenses including rape, indecent exposure or unwanted touching, according to figures released by the Office for National Statistics (ONS).

It said the Crime Survey for England and Wales (CSEW) estimated that 20 percent of women and 4 percent of men have experienced some type of sexual assault since the age of 16, equivalent to 3.4 million female victims and 631,000 male victims.

Many people wish to live or even visit the UK as it is one of the most developed countries. But they surely must not be aware that this country is also involved badly in the crime of rape.

In 2017, the Ministry of Justice (MoJ), Office for National Statistics (ONS) and Home Office released its first ever joint Official Statistics bulletin on sexual violence, entitled An Overview of Sexual Offending in England and Wales. According to report: Approximately 85,000 women are raped on average in England and Wales every year. Over 400,000 women are sexually assaulted each year. One in 5 women (aged 16 – 59) has experienced some form of sexual violence since the age of 16.

Sexual abuse reporting rates, while low in general, is lower than would have been expected for those living within British South Asian communities according to new research by the University of Hull and the University of Roehampton.

Published in The British Journal of Criminology, the research highlights that powerful cultural norms within British South Asian communities are preventing incidences of sexual violence being reported. The research calls for a national training program to be implemented urgently including compulsory education within all schools to help keep women and children in British South Asian Communities safer.

4. INDIA

India's population is currently 1,355,266,764 as of August 2018, based on the latest United Nations estimates. India population is equivalent to 17.74% of the total world population.

Rape is the fourth most common crime against women in India.

According to the National Crime Records Bureau (NCRB) 2013 annual report, 24,923 rape cases were reported across India in 2012. Out of these, 24,470 were committed by someone known to the victim (98% of the cases).

India has been characterized as one of the "countries with the lowest per capita rates of rape". A large number of rapes go unreported.

The willingness to report the rape has increased in recent years after several incidents of rape received widespread media attention and triggered public protest. This led the Government of India to reform its penal code for crimes of rape and sexual assault.

However, India is the place where sexual assault is rapidly increasing. Rape in India is one of India's most common crimes against women. According to the National Crime Records Bureau, 24,923 rape cases were reported across India in 2012, but experts agree that the number of unreported cases of sexual assault brings the total much higher. Out of these, 24,470 were committed by parents/family, relatives, neighbors and other known persons implying that men known to the victim committed 98 percent of reported rapes.

The latest estimates suggest that a new case of rape is reported every 22 minutes in India.

India's attitudes towards women reflect apathy and an acceptance of sexual harassment. The tendency to judge and police what women wear is inseparable from the normalization of sexual harassment: both reflect a broader pattern of social control over women's bodies. We explore this further through responses to the statement: "A husband has the right to discipline his wife." Similar trends emerge. Across India, only about a fifth of respondents disagreed with the statement; 60.6% said they slightly or strongly agreed. Women, again, appear to reinforce patriarchal norms. Perhaps, some women are reluctant to voice their views, while others might endorse the status quo. Either way, prospects for gender equality seem grim.

3. SWEDEN

At 450,295 square kilometers (173,860 sq. mi), Sweden is the third-largest country in the European Union by area. Sweden has a total population of 10.2 million of which 2.4 million has a foreign background. It has a low population density of 22 inhabitants per square kilometer (57/sq. mi).

Sweden has the highest incidence of reported rapes in Europe and one of the highest in the world. One amongst every four women comes out to be the victim of rape in Sweden. By 2010, The Swedish police recorded the highest number of offenses – about 63 per 100,000 inhabitants.

The country has the third-highest rape crime in the world. In 2009 there were 15,700 reported sexual offenses in Sweden, a rise of 8% compared to 2008, of which 5,940 were rape and sexual harassment (including exhibitionism) accounted for 7,590 reports. In April 2009, it was reported that sex crimes had increased by 58% over the previous ten years.

According to a 2017 European Union study, Sweden has one of the highest rates of reported rape in Europe.

As of July 2018, Sweden rewrote its rape law. Rape is now defined as sex without explicit verbal or physical consent. There is no need to prove violent coercion, bringing Sweden into line with nine other Western European countries.

The legal change comes after years of campaigning by women's groups. In 2013, protests erupted across the country when three men were acquitted of raping a 14-year-old girl with a glass bottle. The ruling stated that: "People involved in sexual activities do things naturally to each other's body in a spontaneous way, without asking for consent." The absence of explicit consent, the court ruled, did not constitute rape.

Whether the new law will improve Sweden's meager rape conviction rate remains to be seen. But campaigners argue it signals a step change in addressing sexual violence in the country, and that by promoting conversations about consent it could help to prevent countless assaults.

REAL SELF DEFENSE FOR WOMEN

2. SOUTH AFRICA

With the population rising to over 56 million in 2018, the country has one of the highest rates of rape in the world, with some 65,000 rapes and other sexual assaults reported for the year 2012. The incidence of rape has led to the country being referred to as the "rape capital of the world".

One in three of the 4,000 women questioned by the Community of Information, Empowerment, and Transparency said they had been raped in the past year. More than 25 percent of South African men questioned in a survey published by the Medical Research Council (MRC) admitted to rape; of those, nearly half said they had raped more than one person.

Three out of four of those who had admitted rape indicated that they had attacked for the first time during their teens. South Africa has amongst the highest incidences of child and baby rape in the world. If the rapist is convicted, his prison time would be around 2 years.

International finance magazine The Economist has run a feature uncovering what it calls South Africa's 'disgrace' – laying bare unsettling rape statistics in some regions in South Africa.

The publication cited an anonymous survey conducted in 2016 in Diepsloot – a dense population township north of Johannesburg – where 38% of men (two in five) admitted to having forced a woman into having sex with them.

Extending the questions to broader violence – having beaten or threatened to hurt a woman – the statistic jumps to 54%, almost three in five men.

Even more problematic findings came out of the study, one of which is a widely known problem in South Africa: a large number of rape cases go unreported, and when they are reported, little is done.

According to the study, of over 500 sexual assault cases reported to the Diepsloot police since 2013, only one case led to a conviction. According to The Economist, it is estimated that only one in every nine cases of rape is reported to the police.

Coverage of rape in South Africa has been controversial and notoriously misinformed for many years. This is because of the aforementioned low reporting of rape cases, and poor record keeping and reporting of rape statistics.

Simply put, beyond the official number of cases reported to the SAPS, we do not know the true extent of rape and sexual assault in South Africa.

An infamous – and debunked – statistic quoted by South African actress Charlize Theron, and widely cited in media across the world, was that a woman or child is raped every 26 seconds in South Africa.

The most recent data from the South African Police Service shows that between April 2016 and December 2016, there were 30,069 reported cases of rape – down from 32,161 cases over the same period in 2015.

This data shows that South Africa's rape statistics are double the country's murder rate over this (275 days) period at 53.8 cases per 100,000 people in the country. This equates to one person getting raped every 13 minutes.

South Africa's legal definition of rape is very broad. The act states that "any person ('A') who unlawfully and intentionally commits an act of sexual penetration with a complainant ('B'), without the consent of B, is guilty of the offense of rape". This includes the oral, anal or vaginal penetration of a person with a genital organ, anal or vaginal penetration with an object and the penetration of a person's mouth with the genital organs of an animal.

A rape rate (and crime rates in general) are useful for comparing changes over time, as they allow you to make fair comparisons between different population sizes. This is because – generally – the number of crimes committed will rise as a population increases. The rape rate allows us to see whether rape has increased or decreased in relation to the size of the population.

Without the official data, we have calculated South Africa's annual rape rates from 2008/09 to 2014/15 using Statistics South Africa's mid-year population estimates.

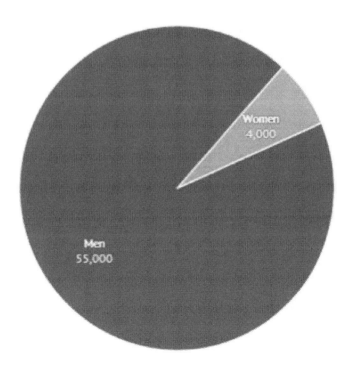

REAL SELF DEFENSE FOR WOMEN

1. UNITED STATES

According to the US Census Bureau's population clock, the estimated 2018 United States population (February 2018) is 327.16 million. This is a bit higher than the 326.77 million estimated by the United Nations.

The superpower of the world is in the first position in the race of rapes. Males are majorly the rapist holding a proportion of 99%. Out of all the victims, 91% are females while 9% are males. The U.S Bureau of Justice Statistics states that 91% of rape victims are female and 9% are male, and nearly 99% of rapists are male.

According to the National Violence Against Women Survey, 1 in 6 U.S. women and 1 in 33 U.S. men have experienced an attempted or completed rape in their lifetime. More than a quarter of college-age women report having experienced a rape or rape attempt since age 14. Out of all, only 16% of the total cases are reported.

Outdoor rape is not common in the USA rather most of the rape cases take place inside homes.

Sexual Assault in the United States

- One in five women and one in 71 men will be raped at some point in their lives.

- In the U.S., one in three women and one in six men experienced some form of contact sexual violence in their lifetime.

- 51.1% of female victims of rape reported being raped by an intimate partner and 40.8% by an acquaintance.

- 52.4% of male victims report being raped by an acquaintance and 15.1% by a stranger.

- Almost half (49.5%) of multiracial women and over 45% of American Indian/Alaska Native women were subjected to some form of contact sexual violence in their lifetime

- 91% of victims of rape and sexual assault are female, and nine percent are male

- In eight out of 10 cases of rape, the victim knew the perpetrator

- Eight percent of rapes occur while the victim is at work

CHAPTER 4

HOW DO YOU FEEL NOW?

Have you ever felt frightened or intimidated when out walking alone? Have you ever wondered what you should do if approached by an attacker? Have you ever worried about becoming yet another home invasion statistic?

The sad reality is that we live in an increasingly violent society in which the fear of crime is ever-present. Personal safety has become an issue of importance for everyone, but especially for women.

The following points are ten things that every woman should know about personal safety,

1. Awareness:

Your first line of defense. Most people think of kicks to the groin and blocking punches when they hear the term "self-defense." However, true self-defense begins long before any actual physical contact. The first, and probably most important, component in self-defense is awareness: awareness of yourself, your surroundings, and your potential attacker's likely strategies.

Violence at school

90,000 children are hospitalized for "intentional" injuries that happened on school grounds every year

GENDER
- 68% males
- 32% females

AGE (YEARS)
- 17% 5-9
- 48% 10-14
- 35% 15-19

TYPE OF INJURY
- contusion/abrasion: 40%
- laceration: 16%
- fractures: 12%
- brain injuries: 10%
- sprains/strains: 7%
- other/unknown: 16%

The criminal's primary strategy is to use the advantage of surprise. Studies have shown that criminals are adept at choosing targets who appear to be unaware of what is going on around them. By being aware of your surroundings and by projecting a "force presence," many altercations which are commonplace on the street can be avoided.

2. Use your sixth sense.

"Sixth sense." "Gut instinct." Whatever you call it, your intuition is a powerful subconscious insight into situations and people. All of us, especially women, have this gift, but very few of us pay attention to it. Learn to trust this power and use it to your full advantage.

Avoid a person or a situation which does not "feel" safe–you're probably right.

3. Self-defense training.

It is important to evaluate the goals and practical usefulness of a women's self-defense program before signing up. Here are two tips:

a) Avoid martial arts studios unless you specifically wish to train in the traditional martial arts techniques and are prepared for a long-term commitment. Many women's self-defense programs teach watered-down martial arts techniques that are complex and unrealistic under the stress of an actual attack;

b) The self-defense program should include simulated assaults, with a fully padded instructor in realistic rape and attack scenarios, to allow you to practice what you've learned.

4. Escape:

Always your best option. What if the unthinkable happens? You are suddenly confronted by a predator who demands that you go with him–be it in a car, or into an alley, or a building. It would seem prudent to obey, but you must never leave the primary crime scene. You are far more likely to be killed or seriously injured if you go with the predator than if you run away (even if he promises not to hurt you). Runaway, yell for help, throw a rock through a store or car window–do whatever you can to attract attention. And if the criminal is after your purse or other material items, throw them one way while you run the other.

5. Your right to fight.

Unfortunately, no matter how diligently we practice awareness and avoidance techniques, we may find ourselves in a physical confrontation. Whether or not you have self-defense training, and no matter what your age or physical condition, it is important to understand that you CAN and SHOULD defend yourself physically. You have both the moral and legal right to do so, even if the attacker is only threatening you and hasn't struck first. Many women worry that they will anger the attacker and get hurt worse if they defend themselves, but statistics clearly show that your odds of survival are far greater if you do fight back. Aim for the eyes first and the groin second. Remember, though, to use the element of surprise to your advantage–strike quickly, and mean business. You may only get one chance.

6. Pepper spray:

Pros and cons. Pepper spray, like other self-defense aids, can be a useful tool. However, it is important to understand that there can be significant drawbacks to its use. For example, did you know that it doesn't work on everyone? Surprisingly, 15-20% of people will not be incapacitated even by a full-face spray. Also, if you're carrying it in your purse, you will only waste time and alert the attacker to your intentions while you fumble for it. Never depend on any self-defense tool or weapon to stop an attacker. Trust your body and your wits, which you can always depend on in the event of an attack.

7. Home invasions:

A crime on the rise. The primary way to prevent a home invasion is simply to never, ever open your door unless you either are certain you know who's on the other side or can verify that they have a legitimate reason for being there (dressing up as a repair person or even police officer is one trick criminals use). In the event that an intruder breaks in while you are home, you should have a safe room in your house to which you can retreat. Such a room should be equipped with a strong door, deadbolt lock, phone (preferably cell phone), and a can of pepper spray or fire extinguisher.

8. Avoiding a car-jacking.

Lock all doors and keep windows up when driving. Most car-jacking take place when vehicles are stopped at intersections. The criminal's approach at a 45-degree angle (in the blind spot), and either pull you out of the driver's seat or jump in the passenger's seat.

9. A travel tip.

Violent crimes against women happen in the best and worst hotels around the world. Predators may play the part of a hotel employee, push their way through an open or unlocked door, or obtain a passkey to the room. As with home safety, never open your door unless you are certain the person on the other side is legitimate, and always carry a door wedge with you when you travel. A wedge is often stronger than the door it secures.

10. Safety in cyberspace.

Although the Internet is educational and entertaining, it can also be full of danger if one isn't careful. When communicating online, use a nickname and always keep personal information such as home address and phone number confidential. Instruct family members to do the same. Keep current on security issues, frauds, viruses, etc. by periodically referring to "The Police Notebook" Internet Safety Page.

REAL SELF DEFENSE FOR WOMEN

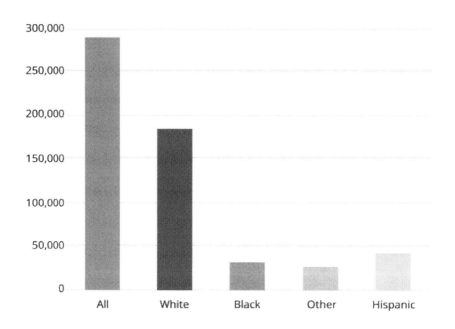

Our research has revealed alarming Australian statistics about violence, and evidence that the problems are increasing. For example:

- 25% of children are physically bullied.
- 40% of youth suicide is caused by bullying.
- Child abduction by strangers is increasing.
- A 128% increase in sexual assaults since 1990.
- 1 in 3 women are sexually or physically assaulted in their lifetime. 35% will become victims of domestic violence.
- Australia has the world's 3rd highest rate per capita for rape.

REAL SELF DEFENSE FOR WOMEN

Domestic violence is the most common cause of death of women aged between 25 and 45.

Everyone should take 5 minutes to read this. It may save your life or a loved one's life. In daylight hours, refresh yourself of these things to do in an emergency situation… This is for you, and for you to share with your wife, your children, & everyone you know. After reading these 9 crucial tips, forward this website to someone you care about. It never hurts to be careful in this crazy world we live in.

10 Personal Safety Tips:

1. Tip for a serious close in attack: The elbow and knees are the strongest point on your body. If you are close enough to use them, do!

2. Learned this from a tourist guide. If a robber asks for your wallet and/or purse, **DO NOT HAND IT TO HIM**. Toss it away from you… Chances are that he is more interested in your wallet and/or purse than you, and he will go for the wallet/purse. **RUN LIKE MAD IN THE OTHER DIRECTION!**

3. If you are ever thrown into the trunk of a car, kick out the back-tail lights and stick your arm out the hole and start waving like crazy. The driver won't see you, but everybody else will. This has saved lives.

4. Women tend to get into their cars after shopping, eating, working, etc., and just sit (doing their checkbook, or making a list, etc. DON'T DO THIS!) The predator will be watching you, and this is the perfect opportunity for him to get in on the passenger side, put a gun to your head, and tell you where to go. **AS SOON AS YOU GET INTO YOUR CAR, LOCK THE DOORS AND LEAVE.**

If someone is in the car with a gun to your head **DO NOT DRIVE OFF, repeat: DO NOT DRIVE OFF!** Instead gun the engine and speed into anything, wrecking the car. Your Air Bag will save you. If the person is in the back seat, they will get the worst of it. As soon as the car crashes bail out and run. It is better than having them find your body in a remote location.

5. A few notes about getting into your car in a parking lot, or parking garage:

A.) Be aware: look around you, look into your car, at the passenger side floor, and in the back seat.

B.) If you are parked next to a big van, enter your car from the passenger door. Most serial killers attack their victims by pulling them into their vans while the women are attempting to get into their cars.

C.) Look at the car parked on the driver's side of your vehicle, and the passenger side. If a male is sitting alone in the seat nearest your car, you may want to walk back into the mall, or work, and get a guard/policeman to walk you back out. **IT IS ALWAYS BETTER TO BE SAFE THAN SORRY.** (And better paranoid than dead.)

6. ALWAYS take the elevator instead of the stairs. Stairwells are horrible places to be alone and the perfect crime spot. This is especially true at NIGHT!).

7. If the predator has a gun and you are not under his control, **ALWAYS RUN!** The predator will only hit you (a running target) 4 in 100 times; and even then, it most likely **WILL NOT** be a vital organ. **RUN**, preferably in a zig-zag pattern!

8. As women, we are always trying to be sympathetic: **STOP** it may get you raped or killed. Ted Bundy, the serial killer, was a good-looking, well-educated man, who **ALWAYS** played on the sympathies of unsuspecting women. He walked with a cane, or a limp, and often asked 'for help' into his vehicle or with his vehicle, which is when he abducted his next victim.

9. Another Safety Point: Someone just told me that her friend heard a crying baby on her porch the night before last, and she called the police because it was late, and she thought it was weird. The police told her 'Whatever you do, **DO NOT** open the door. The lady then said that it sounded like the baby had crawled near a window, and she was worried that it would crawl to the street and get run over. The policeman said, 'We already have a unit on the way, whatever you do, **DO NOT** open the door.' He told her that they think a serial killer has a baby's cry recorded and uses it to coax women out of their homes thinking that someone dropped off a baby. He said they have not verified it but have had several calls by women saying that they hear baby's cries outside their doors when they're home alone at night.

10. Water scam! If you wake up in the middle of the night to hear all your taps outside running or what you think is a burst pipe, **DO NOT GO OUT TO INVESTIGATE!** These people turn on all your outside taps full blast so that you will go out to investigate and then attack.

REAL SELF DEFENSE FOR WOMEN

Stay alert, keep safe, and look out for your neighbors! Please pass this on This e-mail should probably be taken seriously because the Crying Baby Theory was mentioned on America's Most Wanted when they profiled the serial killer in Louisiana.

CHAPTER 5

WHATS IN YOUR WALLET?

Criminals don't always need sawed-off shotguns and ski masks to make a big haul — your social security number, or a pre-approved credit card application from your trash could be all they need.

Identity Theft

Criminals don't always need sawed-off shotguns and ski masks to make a big haul — your social security number, or a pre-approved credit card application from your trash could be all they need.

Identity theft is the nation's fastest-growing crime according to FBI statistics and identity theft/fraud is the fastest-growing category of Federal Trade Commission (FTC) complaints.

Identity theft occurs when someone uses your personally identifying information, like your name, Social Security number, or credit card number, without your permission, to commit fraud or other crimes.

The FTC estimates that as many as 9 million Americans have their identities stolen each year. In fact, you or someone you know may have experienced some form of identity theft. The crime takes many forms. Identity thieves may rent an apartment, obtain a credit card, or establish a telephone account in your name. You may not find out about the theft until you review your credit report or a credit card statement and notice a charge you didn't make—or until you're contacted by a debt collector.

Identity theft is serious. While some identity theft victims can resolve their problems quickly, others spend hundreds of dollars and many days repairing damage to their good name and credit record. Some consumers victimized by identity theft may lose out on job opportunities or be denied loans for education, housing or cars because of negative information on their credit reports. In rare cases, they may even be arrested for crimes they did not commit.

What is identity theft?

"Identity theft" refers to crimes in which someone wrongfully obtains and uses another person's personal data (i.e., name, date of birth, social security number, driver's license number, and your financial identity— credit card, bank account and phone-card numbers) in some way that involves fraud or deception, typically for economic gain (to obtain money or goods/services). Criminals also use identity theft to fraudulently obtain identification cards, driver licenses, birth certificates, social security numbers, travel visas and other official government papers.

Unlike your fingerprints (which are unique to you and can't easily be given to, or stolen by, someone else for their use), your personal data can be used, if it falls into the wrong hands, allowing criminals to profit at your expense. Plus, according to the FTC, —on average, most victims don't even know their identity has been stolen for more than a year later.

Identity theft can have devastating consequences for you, as the victim, who may face long hours of closing bad accounts, opening new ones, and repairing your wrecked credit record. And, it may take significant out-of-pocket expenses to clear your good name. In the meantime, you may be denied jobs, loans, education, housing, and cars, or even get arrested for crimes you didn't commit. Unfortunately, the experience of thousands of victims is that it often requires months, and even years, to navigate the frustrating, identity-recovery process.

How identity thieves GET your personal information:

Identity thieves can use a variety of high/low tech means to gain access to your personal information. Here are some of the ways these imposters can get your personal information and take over your identity —

• Business Record Theft: They get your information from businesses or institutions by stealing files out of offices where you're a customer, employee, patient or student; or bribing an employee who has access to your files, or even "hacking" into the organization's computer files.

• Shoulder Surfing: A "shoulder-surfing" identity thief, standing next to you in a checkout line, can memorize your name, address and phone number during the short time it takes you to write a check. An identity thief can stand near a public phone and watch you punch in your phone or credit card numbers (or even listen in when you give your credit card number over the phone for a hotel room or rental-car.)

• Dumpster Diving: They rummage through your trash, or the trash of businesses, and landfills for personal data.

• Under the Color of Authority: They fraudulently obtain credit reports by abusing their employer's authorized access to credit reports, or by posing as landlords, employers or others who may have a legitimate need/right to the information.

• Skimming: They steal your credit/debit card account numbers as your card is processed at a restaurant, store or other business location, using a special data collection/storage device (known as "skimmer".)

Other forms of old-fashioned fraud and theft –

- Stealing wallets and purses containing identification and credit and bank cards.

- Stealing mail, including bank and credit card statements, pre-approved credit offers, new checks, or tax information.

- Completing a "change of address form" to divert your mail to another location.

- Stealing personal information from your home.

- Using the personal information, you share on the Internet.

- Scamming information from you, often through email, by posing as legitimate companies or government agencies.

How identity thieves USE your personal information:

- Go on spending sprees using your credit and debit card account numbers to buy "big-ticket" items like computers that they can easily sell.

- Open a new credit card account, using your name, date of birth and SSN. When they use the credit card and don't pay the bills, the delinquent account is reported on your credit report.

- Call your credit card issuer and, pretending to be you, ask to change the mailing address on your credit card account. The imposter then runs up charges on your account. Because your bills are being sent to the new address, it may take some time before you realize there's a problem.

REAL SELF DEFENSE FOR WOMEN

- Buy cars by taking out auto loans in your name.

- Establish a phone or wireless service in your name.

- Counterfeit checks or debit cards and drain your bank account.

- Open a bank account in your name and write bad checks on that account.

- File for bankruptcy under your name to avoid paying debts they've incurred under your name, or to avoid eviction.

- Give your name to the police during an arrest. If they're released from police custody, but don't show up for their court date, an arrest warrant is issued in your name.

Total Fraud Victims Reaches Record High

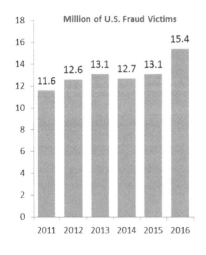
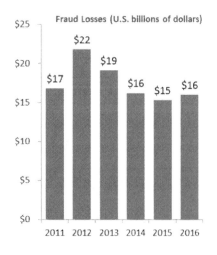

How can I tell if I'm a victim of identity theft?

Monitor the balances of your financial accounts – Look for unexplained charges or withdrawals.

- Other indications of identity theft include:
- Failing to receive bills or other mail, which may signal an address change by the identity thief.
- Receiving credit cards, and/or statements of accounts, for which you did not apply.
- A lender tries to repossess a car you didn't know you owned.
- Being contacted by the police after a crime is committed in your name.
- Being denied credit for no apparent reason.

If you're ever denied credit, FIND OUT WHY, especially if you haven't reviewed your credit report lately. This may be the first indication you get that someone has stolen your identity and is racking up charges in your name.

• Receiving calls or letters from debt collectors or businesses about merchandise or services you did not buy.

• REACT QUICKLY if a creditor or merchant calls you about charges you didn't make. This, too, may be the first notice you get that someone has stolen your identity. Get as much information from them as you can and investigate immediately.

What are the steps I should take if I'm a victim of identity theft?

1. Place a fraud alert on your credit reports and review your credit reports.

Fraud alerts can help prevent an identity thief from opening any more accounts in your name. Contact the toll-free fraud number of any of the three consumer reporting companies below to place a fraud alert on your credit report. You only need to contact one of the three companies to place an alert. The company you call is required to contact the other two, which will place an alert on their versions of your report, too. If you do not receive a confirmation from a company, you should contact that company directly to place a fraud alert.

- TransUnion: 1-800-680-7289; www.transunion.com; Fraud Victim Assistance Division, P.O. Box 6790, Fullerton, CA 92834-6790
- Equifax: 1-800-525-6285; www.equifax.com; P.O. Box 740241, Atlanta, GA 30374-0241
- Experian: 1-888-EXPERIAN (397-3742) www.experian.com; P.O. Box 9554, Allen, TX 75013

2. Close the accounts that you know, or believe, have been tampered with or opened fraudulently.

Call and speak with someone in the security or fraud department of each company. Follow up in writing and include copies (NOT originals) of supporting documents. It's important to notify credit card companies and banks in writing. Send your letters by certified mail, return receipt requested, so you can document what the company received and when. Keep a file of your correspondence and enclosures.

3. File a complaint with the Federal Trade Commission.

You can file a complaint with the FTC using the online complaint form; or call the FTC's Identity Theft Hotline, toll-free: 1-877-ID-theft (438-4338); TTY: 1-866-653-4261; or write Identity Theft Clearinghouse, Federal Trade Commission, 600 Pennsylvania Avenue, NW, Washington, DC 20580. Be sure to call the Hotline to update your complaint if you have any additional information or problems.

4. File a report with your local police or the police in the community where the identity theft took place.

Call your local police department and tell them that you want to file a report about your identity theft. Ask them if you can file the report in person. If you cannot, ask if you can file a report over the Internet or telephone. See below for information about Automated Reports.

If the police are reluctant to take your report, ask to file a "Miscellaneous Incident" report, or try another jurisdiction, like your state police. You also can check with your state Attorney General's office to find out if state law requires the police to take reports for identity theft. Check the Blue Pages of your telephone directory for the phone number or check www.naag.org for a list of state Attorneys General.

Harassing & Obscene Communications

Anyone can be the victim of harassing, annoying, obscene or threatening telephone calls, email, text messages, and other communications. Although such calls/messages do not usually constitute a threat to personal safety, on-campus residents should contact OUPD, and off-campus residents should contact the Norman Police Department, on receipt of a telephone call of questionable intent or origin. They can usually help you stop the unwanted communications.

Online Cyberstalking

National surveys indicate that there is a tremendous increase in cyberstalking incidents among college women.

Cyberstalking is threatening or harassing behavior directed at another using the Internet or other forms of online and computer communications. Victims can be targeted through chat rooms, message boards, discussion forums and social networking sites. This type of harassment is a misuse of OU computing resources and a violation of the Student Code.

Victims should consider filing a report of any harassing behavior with OUPD.

The National "DO NOT CALL" Registry

The National Do Not Call Registry gives you a choice about whether to receive telemarketing calls at home. Most telemarketers should not call your number once it has been on the registry for 31 days. If they do, you can file a complaint at this website. You can register your home or mobile phone for free.
Your registration will not expire. Telephone numbers placed on the National Do Not Call Registry will remain on it permanently due to the Do-Not-Call Improvement Act of 2007, which became law in February 2008.

Scammers have been making phone calls claiming to represent the National Do Not Call Registry. The calls claim to provide an opportunity to sign up for the Registry. These calls are not coming from the Registry or the Federal Trade Commission, and you should not respond to these calls. To add your number to the Registry you can call 888-382-1222 from the phone you wish to register.

Preventing Identity Theft

While nothing can guarantee that you won't become a victim of identity theft, you can minimize your risk, and minimize the damage if a problem develops, by making it more difficult for identity thieves to access your personal information.

Protect your Social Security number

Don't carry your Social Security card in your wallet or write your Social Security number on a check. Give your Social Security number only when absolutely necessary and ask to use other types of identifiers. If your state uses your Social Security number as your driver's license number, ask to substitute another number. Do the same if your health insurance company uses your Social Security number as your policy number.

Your employer and financial institutions will need your Social Security number for wage and tax reporting purposes. Other businesses may ask you for your Social Security number to do a credit check if you are applying for a loan, renting an apartment, or signing up for utilities. Sometimes, however, they simply want your Social Security number for general record keeping. If someone asks for your Social Security number, ask:

- Why do you need my Social Security number?

- How will my Social Security number be used?

- How do you protect my Social Security number from being stolen?

- What will happen if I don't give you my Social Security number?

If you don't provide your Social Security number, some businesses may not provide you with the service or benefit you want. Getting satisfactory answers to these questions will help you decide whether you want to share your Social Security number with the business. The decision to share is yours.

Treat your trash and mail carefully

To thwart an identity thief who may pick through your trash or recycling bins to capture your personal information, always shred your charge receipts, copies of credit applications, insurance forms, physician statements, checks and bank statements, expired charge cards that you're discarding, and credit offers you get in the mail.

Deposit your outgoing mail containing personally identifying information in post office collection boxes or at your local post office, rather than in an unsecured mailbox. Promptly remove mail from your mailbox. If you're planning to be away from home and can't pick up your mail, contact the U.S. Postal Service at 1-800-275-8777 or online at www.usps.gov, to request a vacation hold. The Postal Service will hold your mail at your local post office until you can pick it up or are home to receive it.

Be on guard when using the Internet

The Internet can give you access to information, entertainment, financial offers, and countless other services but at the same time, it can leave you vulnerable to online scammers, identity thieves and more. For practical tips to help you be on guard against Internet fraud, secure your computer, and protect your personal information,

Select intricate passwords

Place passwords on your credit card, bank, and phone accounts. Avoid using easily available information like your mother's maiden name, your birth date, the last four digits of your Social Security number or your phone number, a series of consecutive numbers, or a single word that would appear in a dictionary. Combinations of letters, numbers, and special characters make the strongest passwords. When opening new accounts, you may find that many businesses still ask for your mother's maiden name. Find out if you can use a password instead.

Verify a source before sharing information

Don't give out personal information on the phone, through the mail, or on the Internet unless you've initiated the contact and are sure you know whom you're dealing with. Identity thieves are clever and may pose as representatives of banks, Internet service providers (ISPs), and even government agencies to get people to reveal their Social Security number, mother's maiden name, account numbers, and other identifying information.

Before you share any personal information, confirm that you are dealing with a legitimate organization. Many companies post scam alerts when their name is used improperly. Or call customer service using the number listed on your account statement or in the telephone book.

Safeguard your purse and wallet

Protect your purse and wallet at all times. Don't carry your Social Security number or card; leave it in a secure place. Carry only the identification information and the credit and debit cards that you'll actually need when you go out.

Store information in secure locations

Keep your personal information in a secure place at home, especially if you have roommates, employ outside help, or are having work done in your house. Share your personal information only with those family members who have a legitimate need for it. Keep your purse or wallet in a safe place at work; do the same with copies of administrative forms that have your sensitive personal information.

Ask about information security procedures in your workplace or at businesses, doctor's offices or other institutions that collect your personally identifying information. Find out who has access to your personal information and verify that it is handled securely. Ask about the disposal procedures for those records as well. Find out if your information will be shared with anyone else. If so, ask how your information can be kept confidential.

Limit, protect, and be aware of the type and amount of personal data you carry around...

Keep your purse/wallet and organizer/briefcase - as well as any copies you may retain of administrative forms that contain your sensitive personal information - in a safe place at work.

Carry only the identification information and the number of credit and debit cards that you'll actually need. Don't carry any critical identification documents in your wallet, like your birth certificate or passport, unless absolutely necessary for a specific immediate task/purpose.

Don't make your wallet a long-term financial file-cabinet of bank receipts, invoices, etc. —Take time to remove such items from your wallet each day.

Use care and consider what sensitive personal information you carry around in a paper/loose-leaf or electronic organizer, briefcase, or another device/container/method.

Coping with lost or stolen wallets

Always assume your wallet has been stolen if you can't locate it after a reasonable search - far better to report a theft and have to cancel the report than to assume the wallet is misplaced and have to deal with the use and misuse of your identity and credit

Coping with a lost/stolen wallet will be easier if you have previously photocopied both sides of everything in your wallet (driver license, credit cards, membership cards, etc.)Keep the copies in a safe but readily accessible place. You can also download/print our "Lost/Stolen Wallet Inventory & Emergency Checklist" to record the key information from your wallet contents, then store the list a safe place.

File a police report where the wallet was stolen. It establishes a record to combat fraud.

While you should never carry your original Social Security card or even just the number in your wallet, consider reporting the theft of your wallet to the Social Security Administration fraud line: 1-800-269-0271. This will prevent or greatly impede the thief from obtaining a replacement card using the identity information from your wallet.
Don't ONLY contact the credit-card providers of the credit cards you had in your wallet; also notify the three major credit agencies to put a fraud alert on your credit report. By doing this, purchases made in your name usually won't hurt your credit rating, and the thief might not be issued credit without you being contacted.

• Place passwords on your credit card, bank, brokerage and phone accounts. Avoid using easily available information like your mother's maiden name, your birth date, the last four digits of your SSN or your phone number, or a series of consecutive numbers. When opening new accounts, you may find that many businesses still have a line on their applications for your mother's maiden name. Use a password instead.

• Ask about information security procedures in your workplace or at businesses, doctor's offices or other institutions that collect personally identifying information from you. Find out who can access your personal information and verify that it is handled and stored securely. Ask about the disposal procedures for those records as well. Find out if your information will be shared with anyone else. If so, ask if you can keep your information confidential.

What is a credit freeze?

Many states have laws that let consumers "freeze" their credit – in other words, letting a consumer restrict access to his or her credit report. If you place a credit freeze, potential creditors and other third parties will not be able to get access to your credit report unless you temporarily lift the freeze. This means that it's unlikely that an identity thief would be able to open a new account in your name. Placing a credit freeze does not affect your credit score – nor does it keep you from getting your free annual credit report, or from buying your credit report or score.

Credit freeze laws vary from state to state. In some states, anyone can freeze their credit file, while in other states, only identity theft victims can. The cost of placing, temporarily lifting and removing a credit freeze also varies. Many states make credit freezes free for identity theft victims, while other consumers pay a fee – typically $10. It's also important to know that these costs are for each of the credit reporting agencies. If you want to freeze your credit, it would mean placing the freeze with each of three credit reporting agencies and paying the fee to each one.

Who can access my credit report if I place a credit freeze?

If you place a credit freeze, you will continue to have access to your free annual credit report. You'll also be able to buy your credit report and credit score even after placing a credit freeze. Companies that you do business with will still have access to your credit report – for example, your mortgage, credit card, or cell phone company – as would collection agencies that are working for one of those companies. Companies will also still be able to offer you prescreened credit. Those are the credit offers you receive in the mail that you have not applied for. Additionally, in some states, potential employers, insurance companies, landlords, and other non-creditors can still get access to your credit report with a credit freeze in place.

Can I temporarily lift my credit freeze if I need to let someone check my credit report?

If you want to apply for a loan or credit card, or otherwise need to give someone access to your credit report and that person is not covered by an exception to the credit freeze law, you would need to temporarily lift the credit freeze. You would do that by using a PIN that each credit reporting agency would send once you placed the credit freeze. In most states, you'd have to pay a fee to lift the credit freeze. Most states currently give the credit reporting agencies three days to lift the credit freeze. This might keep you from getting "instant" credit, which may be something to weigh when considering a credit freeze.

What does a credit freeze not do?

While a credit freeze can help keep an identity thief from opening most new accounts in your name, it's not a solution to all types of identity theft. It will not protect you, for example, from an identity thief who uses your existing credit cards or other accounts. There are also new accounts, such as telephone, wireless, and bank accounts, which an ID thief could open without a credit check. In addition, some creditors might open an account without first getting your credit report. And, if there's identity theft already going on when you place the credit freeze, the freeze itself won't be able to stop it. While a credit freeze may not protect you in these kinds of cases, it can protect you from the vast majority of identity theft that involves opening a new line of credit.

What's the difference between a credit freeze and a fraud alert?

A fraud alert is another tool for people who've had their ID stolen – or who suspect it may have been stolen. With a fraud alert in place, businesses may still check your credit report. Depending on whether you place an initial 90-day fraud alert or an extended fraud alert, potential creditors must either contact you or use what the law refers to as "reasonable policies and procedures" to verify your identity before issuing credit in your name. However, the steps potential creditors take to verify your identity may not always alert them that the applicant is not you.

A credit freeze, on the other hand, will prevent potential creditors and other third parties from accessing your credit report at all, unless you lift the freeze or already have a relationship with the company. Some consumers use credit freezes because they feel they give more protection. As with credit freezes, fraud alerts are mainly effective against new credit accounts being opened in your name but will likely not stop thieves from using your existing accounts or opening new accounts such as new telephone or wireless accounts, where credit is often not checked. Also, only people who've had their ID stolen – or who suspect it may have been stolen, may place fraud alerts. In some states, anyone can place a credit freeze.

About identity theft insurance

Although identity theft insurance won't deter identity thieves, it can, in certain circumstances, minimize losses if an identity theft occurs. As with any product or service, as you consider whether to buy, be sure you understand what you'd be getting. Things to consider include: (1) the amount of coverage the policy provides; (2) whether it covers any lost wages (and, if so, whether there's a cap on the wages you can claim or a separate deductible); (3) the amount of the deductible; (4) what might be excluded (for example, if the thief is a family member or if the thief made electronic withdrawals and transfers); (5) whether the policy provides a personal counselor to help you resolve the problems of identity theft; and (6) whether your existing homeowner's policy already contains some coverage. Be aware that one of the major "costs" of identity theft is the time you will spend to clear your name.

Also, be aware that many companies and law enforcement officers will only deal with you (as opposed to an insurance company representative). So, even if your policy provides you with a personal counselor, that counselor can often only guide you, as opposed to doing the work to clear your name. And, as you evaluate insurance products and services, you may also consider checking out the insurer with your local Better Business Bureau, consumer protection agency, and state Attorney General.

Currently, the FBI is releasing the 2017 edition of its annual report Crime in the United States, a statistical compilation of offense, arrest, and police employee data reported voluntarily by law enforcement agencies that participate in the Bureau's Uniform Crime Reporting (UCR) Program. This latest report reveals that the estimated number of violent crimes reported by law enforcement to UCR's Summary Reporting System during 2017 decreased 0.2 percent when compared with 2016 data. And the estimated number of property crimes decreased 4.3 percent from 2016 levels.

Here are some highlights from Crime in the United States,

- There were an estimated 1,165,383 violent crimes (murder and non-negligent homicides, rapes, robberies, and aggravated assaults) reported by law enforcement.
- Aggravated assaults accounted for 63.6 percent of the violent crimes reported, while robberies accounted for 28.0 percent, rape 7.2 percent, and murders 1.2 percent.
- There were an estimated 8,277,829 property crimes (burglaries, larceny-thefts, and motor vehicle thefts) reported by law enforcement. Financial losses suffered by victims of these crimes were calculated at approximately $14.3 billion.
- Larceny-theft accounted for 70.8 percent of all property crimes reported, burglary for 20.9 percent, and motor vehicle theft for 8.3 percent
- Police made an estimated 11,205,833 arrests during 2014—498,666 for violent crimes, and 1,553,980 for property crimes. More than 73 percent of those arrested during 2014 were male.
- The highest number of arrests was for drug abuse violations (1,561,231), followed by larceny-theft (1,238,190) and driving under the influence (1,117,852).

CHAPTER 6

WHATS NEW?

REAL SELF DEFENSE FOR WOMEN

When I first began writing this book my foremost thought was to enlist the best-qualified authorities on the subject matter. In correlation to that end, I contacted the Federal Bureau of Investigations for their assistance in this matter. The response was more than satisfactory, and I was amazed at the candid acceptance of my request as well as the personal contact directly from the F.B.I. head official in charge of such information.

James Comey, at the time of this request, was the acting Director of the F.B.I. and one of the foremost authorities on security and defense in the United States of America. With his assistance and support, I was able to gain a much deeper insight into the levels and degree that violence against women happened in the U.S.A.

I was stunned and shocked at the statistics and information forwarded to me but also grateful for the unparalleled access to the information he shared with me. I could not foresee hiding this information and not relating it forward to the reader. In my opinion, it is one of the most valuable resources put together to show a clear line of behaviors adjacent to the activities of violence against women.

Whatever your political leanings are and regardless of the thrust of media attention he has garnered over the course of his tenure at the F.B.I. he has faithfully served his nation as an outstanding individual in Law Enforcement and its service.

James Comey Born in Yonkers, New York in 1960, began his rise as a government prosecutor after graduating from the University of Chicago Law School in 1985. He was appointed U.S. attorney for the Southern District of New York in 2001, and in 2003 he became deputy attorney general. In 2013, Comey was confirmed as director of the FBI. However, he became embroiled in controversy due to the investigation of 2016 presidential candidates Hillary Clinton and Donald Trump, leading to his termination by President Trump in May 2017.

His time as the Director of the F.B.I. was an asset to the information gained for the writing of this book and without it, I do not feel that I could not have painted a better graphic for the reader accurately.

In a recent report by New York Times reporter Emily Steel on the Comey hearings in the Senate in Washington D.C. in mid-2018, his testimony was seen akin to that of a sexual harassment-assault.

Emily Steel, who is a business journalist who has covered the media industry at The New York Times since 2014. Along with a team of reporters who exposed sexual harassment and misconduct across several industries, was awarded a Pulitzer Prize for public service in 2018.

Ms. Steel's reporting at the Comey hearings noted that for some people who watched James B. Comey's Senate testimony in July 2018, the questions that Mr. Comey, the former F.B.I. director faced and the situations he described brought to mind a seemingly unrelated topic: sexual harassment.

As members of the Senate Intelligence Committee questioned Mr. Comey, sometimes sharply, asking why he did not immediately report any behavior by President Trump that he thought was inappropriate, why he did not quit as F.B.I. director and why he continued to take private calls from Mr. Trump even after he was unnerved by their one-on-one interactions, commentators on social media made comparisons to the difficulties and doubts faced by women who have been sexually harassed or abused.

Comey stated clearly in his testimony to Congress, "Maybe if I were stronger, I would have" pushed back, Comey said. "I was so stunned by the conversation that I just took it in."

For anyone who was watching, the testimony underscored how sexual harassment is more about power than sex.

Therein lies a tighter connection to the information given. Regardless of how one may interpret the politico, this may fall in to. It reaches out to a larger message about sexual harassment and assaults more than anyone outside the circle of understanding and I personally thank him for his service and his support in forwarding this information to those who need it most.

Forward is a personal note on the subject of violence against women and its perception and effect in America.

A Message from the former FBI Director. Included in the report is a message from former FBI Director James Comey, who said that UCR plans to begin collecting data about non-fatal shootings between law enforcement and civilians, and he encouraged all law enforcement agencies to submit their data about fatal shootings and justifiable homicide data, which is currently collected. Once the FBI begins collecting the expanded data, UCR plans to add a special publication that will focus on law enforcement's use of force in shooting incidents. That report will outline facts about what happened, who was involved, whether there were injuries or deaths, and the circumstances surrounding the incidents.

Explains Comey, "We hope this information will become part of a balanced dialogue in communities and in the media—a dialogue that will help to dispel misperceptions, foster accountability, and promote transparency in how law enforcement personnel relate to the communities they serve."

In his message, James Comey also encourages law enforcement agencies to participate in UCR's National Incident-Based Reporting System (NIBRS), created to improve the quantity and quality of crime data collected by law enforcement by capturing more detailed information on each single crime occurrence.

REAL SELF DEFENSE FOR WOMEN

What's new this year?

For one, this 2019 publication includes the inaugural Federal Crime Data report, which contains traditional UCR data from a handful of federal agencies, as well as FBI arrest data on human trafficking, hate crimes, and criminal computer intrusions.

Also included for the first time in Crime in the United States is UCR's second report of human trafficking data submitted by state and local law enforcement.

It is expected that law enforcement participation in data collection for both reports will expand over time, which will help provide a more complete picture of those crimes.

Recently, the International Association of Chiefs of Police—with the Major Cities Chiefs Association, National Sheriffs' Association, and the Major County Sheriffs' Association—released a paper supporting the adoption of the NIBRS to replace the Summary Reporting System. The group says that the NIBRS "provides a more comprehensive view of crime in the United States and offers greater flexibility in data compilation and analysis."

Beginning in January 2016, data collection began for the newest UCR Program initiative—animal cruelty offenses—requested by the National Sheriffs' Association and the Animal Welfare Institute.

Rape in the United States is defined by the Department of Justice as "Penetration, no matter how slight, of the vagina or anus with any body part or object, or oral penetration by a sex organ of another person, without the consent of the victim." While definitions and terminology of rape vary by jurisdiction in the United States, the FBI revised its definition to eliminate a requirement that the crime involves an element of force.

A 2015 study found that rape is grossly underreported in the United States. Furthermore, a 2016 research paper that compared correlations in murder and rape rates determined those police departments in about 22% of the 210 American cities examined in the study eliminate or undercount rapes from official records in part to "create the illusion of success in fighting violent crime".

Based on the available data, 21.8% of American rapes of female victims are gang rapes. For the last reported year, 2017, the prevalence rate for all sexual assaults including rape was 0.1% (prevalence represents the number of victims, rather than the number of assaults since some are victimized more than once during the reporting period). The survey included males and females aged 12+.

Since rape is a subset of all sexual assaults, the prevalence of rape is lower than the combined statistic. Of those assaults, the Bureau of Justice Statistics stated that 34.8% were reported to the police, up from 29.3% in 2010.

In the United States, at the Federal level, the FBI's Uniform Crime Report (UCR) definitions are used when collating national crime statistics from states across the US. The UCR's definition of rape was changed on January 1, 2013, to remove the requirement of force against a female and to include a wider range of types of penetration.

[1] The new definition reads: "Penetration, no matter how slight, of the vagina or anus with any body part or object, or oral penetration by a sex organ of another person, without the consent of the victim."

At the state level, there is no uniform legal definition of rape; instead, each state has their own laws. These definitions can vary considerably, but many use the term sexual assault, criminal sexual conduct, sexual abuse, sexual battery, etc.
One legal definition is found in the United States Uniform Code of Military Justice [Title 10, Subtitle A, Chapter 47X, Section 920, Article 120], defines rape as:

> (a) Rape. — Any person subject to this chapter who commits a sexual act upon another person by —

(1) Using unlawful force against that other person;

(2) Using force causing or likely to cause death or grievous bodily harm to any person;

(3) Threatening or placing that other person in fear that any person will be subjected to death, grievous bodily harm, or kidnapping;

(4) First rendering that other person unconscious; or

(5) administering to that other person by force or threat of force, or without the knowledge or consent of that person, a drug, intoxicant, or other similar substance and thereby substantially

impairing the ability of that other person to appraise or control conduct; is guilty of rape and shall be punished as a court-martial may direct.

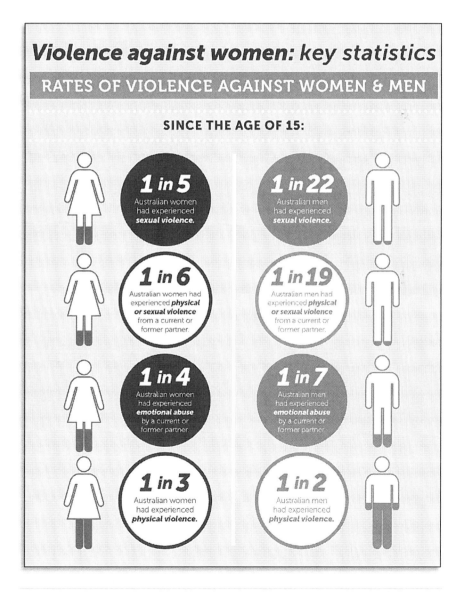

Statistics and data

According to United States Department of Justice document Criminal Victimization in the United States, there were overall 184,610 victims of rape or sexual assault, or 0.1% of the US population 12 or older in 2017.

While the Department of Justice does not publish a report on the breakout of rape vs. other kinds of sexual assault across the total US population, it does provide that level of detail in a related study of college-aged women. The DOJ's Bureau of Justice Statistics indicated that among college women (aged 18–24) women who reported any kind of sexual assault, completed rape represented 38% of incidents between 1995 and 2017.

The Federal Bureau of Investigation have also collected data cases involving victims and perpetrators of rape:

FBI sex offense victims in 2017:

- 73,354 female
- 13,200 male.

FBI convicted sex offenders in 2017:

- 82,500 male
- 6174 female.

Rape in college has also been documented. 2017 data from US Department of Justice, quote:

Rape or sexual assault victimization against females ages 18 to 24, by post-secondary enrollment status, 1995–2017:

Categories	Student victim	Non-student victims
Total	43,302	72,668
Completed rape	12,237	29,369
Attempted rape	9,864	17,792
Sexual assault	10,714	22,260
Threat of rape / assault	5,488	7,247

The mean annual population was 5,130,004 for students and 8,614,853 for non-students.

Demographics

Rape prevalence among women in the U.S. (the percentage of women who experienced rape at least once in their lifetime so far) is in the range of 15–20%, with different studies, disagreeing with each other. (National Violence against Women survey, 1995, found 17.6% prevalence rate; a 2017 national study for the Department of Justice on rape found 19% prevalence rate.

According to a March 2013 report from the U.S. Department of Justice's Bureau of Justice Statistics, from 1995 to 2010, the estimated annual rate of female rape or sexual assault declined 58%, from 5.0 victimizations per 1,000 females age 12 or older to 2.1 per 1,000. Assaults on young women aged 12–17 declined from 11.3 per 1,000 in 1994-1998 to 4.1 per 1,000 in 2005-2010; assaults on women aged 18–34 also declined over the same period, from 7.0 per 1,000 to 3.7.

Most rape research and reporting to date has concentrated on male-female forms of rape. Male-male and female-male rape has not been as thoroughly researched, and almost no research has been done on female-female rape. Emily Young, argues that, if being "made to penetrate" another person is classified as rape rather than as sexual assault, the 12-month prevalence of rape among males is similar to the rate among females.

A 1997 report by the U.S. Bureau of Justice Statistics found that 91% of rape victims are female and 9% are male and that 99% of arrestees for rape are male. However, these statistics are based on reports of "forced penetration". This number excludes instances where men were "made to penetrate" another person, which are assessed separately under "sexual violence". Denov (2004) states that societal responses to the issue of female perpetrators of sexual assault "point to a widespread denial of women as potential sexual aggressors that could work to obscure the true dimensions of the problem."

A 2014 study of rape statistics by the BJS found that 63% of reported rapes against females aged 18 to 24 are done by white males in post-secondary enrollment. The National Violence Against Women Survey found that 34% of American Indian female respondents had experienced attempted or completed rape in their lifetime. The rapist was more likely to be a non-native than a Native.

The 2010 National Intimate Partner and Sexual Violence Survey found that 13.1% of lesbians, 46.1% of bisexual women, and 17.4% of heterosexual women have been raped, physically assaulted, or stalked.

Over the last 4 decades, rape has been declining. According to the National Crime Victimization Survey, the adjusted per-capita victimization rate of rape has declined from about 2.4 per 1000 people (age 12 and above) in 1980 (that is, 2.4 persons from each 1000 people 12 and older were raped during that year) to about 0.4 per 1000 people, a decline of about 85%. There are several possible explanations for this, including stricter laws, education on security for women, and a correlation with the rise in Internet pornography. But other government surveys, such as the Sexual Victimization of College Women study, critique the NCVS on the basis it includes only those acts perceived as crimes by the victim, and report a much higher victimization rate.

Surveys like the NCVS cited above strive to measure rapes that do not get reported to authorities or prosecuted. Some official reports under-represent the prevalence of rape because a significant number of rapes go unreported or do not advance to prosecution.

Rapes and Sexual Assaults are rarely reported to law enforcement. A 2014 report by the Department of Justice showed that only 34.8% of cases of sexual assaults are reported to the authorities.

Definitions of rape can vary, and since not all rapes are reported, researchers instead rely on surveys of student and nonstudent populations to develop a more comprehensive understanding of the prevalence. Survey design including the questions and the sample quality and scope can also create wide ranges in rates.

The most recent study, conducted by the U.S. Department of Justice's Bureau of Justice Statistics, represents a longitudinal study of US women from 1995 to 2013. For the year 2013, the study found that college-aged women (regardless of enrollment status) were more likely to be sexually assaulted at 4.3 per 1,000 (0.4%) and then other women at 1.4 per 1,000 (0.1%). The study also found that the rate of sexual assault has been falling steadily since 1995, from a peak of 0.9% in 1997 to the current 0.4%. Rape, a subset of all sexual assault, had an incidence of 1.4 per 1,000 female students (0.1%) in 2013

In an effort to prevent rape on campuses, the Obama administration has instituted policies requiring schools to investigate rape cases and adjudicate rape cases under a "preponderance of the evidence" standard. These policies have been sharply criticized by civil libertarians concerned that they are eroding due process and will lead to wrongful convictions of the innocent. A number of lawsuits have been filed against colleges and universities by students claiming to have been wrongfully expelled for a rape they did not commit.

Criminal punishment

In the United States, the principle of dual sovereignty applies to rape, as to other crimes. If the rape is committed within the borders of a state, that state has jurisdiction. If the victim is a federal official, an ambassador, consul, or another foreign official under the protection of the United States, or if the crime took place on federal property or involved crossing state borders, or in a manner that substantially affects interstate commerce or national security, then the federal government also has jurisdiction.

If a crime is not committed within any state, such as in the District of Columbia or on a naval or U.S.-flagged merchant vessel in international waters, then federal jurisdiction is exclusive. In cases where the rape involves both state and federal jurisdictions, the offender can be tried and punished separately for each crime without raising issues of double jeopardy.

Because the United States comprises 51 jurisdictions, each with its own criminal code, this section treats only the crime of rape in the federal courts and does not deal with state-by-state specifics. Federal law does not use the term "rape". Rape is grouped with all forms of non-consensual sexual acts under chapter 109a of the United States Code (18 U.S.C. §§ 2241–2248).

Under federal law, the punishment for rape can range from a fine to life imprisonment. The severity of the punishment is based on the use of violence, the age of the victim, and whether drugs or intoxicants were used to override consent. If the perpetrator is a repeat offender, the law prescribes automatically doubling the maximum sentence.

Kennedy v. Louisiana, 554 U.S. (2008) was a decision by the U.S. Supreme Court that held that the Eighth Amendment's cruel and unusual punishment clause did not permit a state to punish the crime of rape of a child with the death penalty if the victim does not die and death was not intended, therefore if a person is convicted of rape he or she is not eligible for the death penalty according to the U.S. Supreme Court's ruling in Kennedy v. Louisiana 554 U.S. (2008).

Different categorizations and maximum punishments for rape under federal law a list of rape laws by state

Treatment of rape victims

Insurance companies have denied coverage for rape victims, claiming a variety of bases for their actions. In one case, after a victim mentioned she had previously been raped 17 years before, an insurance company refused to pay for her rape exam and also refused to pay for therapy or medication for trauma, because she "had been raped before" – indicating a preexisting condition. Some insurance companies have allegedly denied sexual-assault victims mental-health treatment, stating that the service is not medically necessary.

The 2005 Violence Against Women Act requires states to ensure that victims receive access to a forensic examination free of charge regardless of whether the victim chooses to report a sexual assault to law enforcement or cooperate with the criminal justice system. All states must comply with the VAWA 2005 requirement regarding forensic examination in order to receive STOP Violence Against Women Formula Grant Program (STOP Program) funds. Under 42 U.S.C. § 3796gg-4, a State is not entitled to funds under the STOP Program unless the State or another governmental entity "incurs the full out-of-pocket cost of forensic medical exams ... for victims of sexual assault." This means that, if no other governmental entity or insurance carrier pays for the exam, states are required to pay for forensic exams if they wish to receive STOP Program funds.

The goal of this provision is to ensure that the victim is not required to pay for the exam. The effect of the VAWA 2005 forensic examination requirement is to allow victims time to decide whether to pursue their case. Because a sexual assault is a traumatic event, some victims are unable to decide whether they want to cooperate with law enforcement in the immediate aftermath of a sexual assault.

Because forensic evidence can be lost as time progresses, such victims should be encouraged to have the evidence collected as soon as possible without deciding to initiate a report. This provision ensures victims receive timely medical treatment.

Due to bureaucratic mismanagement in some areas, and various loopholes, the victim is sometimes sent a bill anyway, and has difficulty in getting it fixed.

In a more recent report by columnist Laura Finley of New York's ARTVOICE publication, she wrote in her article that the U.S. is divided on political issues is old news. Both the Left and the Right are deeply entrenched, resulting in distrust, animosity, and political gridlock. One troubling example is with the Violence Against Women Act (VAWA) Reauthorization of 2018. Sadly, it isn't the first time that politicians on both sides have attempted to block VAWA, literally using women's lives as a bartering tool.

The original VAWA was introduced by Senator Joe Biden in 1990. It took four years before VAWA passed Congress with bipartisan support and was signed by President Bill Clinton. This is in large part due to a provision that allowed victims the private civil rights remedy of suing their attackers. Chief Justice William Rehnquist was a vocal opponent, asserting that the provision would bring so many cases before the courts it would overwhelm them, and the Supreme Court declared that portion of VAWA to be unconstitutional in 2000. Interestingly, the Court said that Congress did not have the right to enforce the civil remedy under the Commerce Clause because domestic violence is not "economic" in nature, despite evidence that it costs taxpayers between $5-10 billion a year in healthcare and law enforcement costs, lost productivity, and more. Yet the other provisions remained, and VAWA has helped hundreds of thousands of victims. It provides funds for training law enforcement, court officials, victim advocates and healthcare professionals.

VAWA was reauthorized again in 2000 and 2005. The 2000 version improved provisions for immigrant victims, victims of sexual assault, stalking, and dating violence. The 2005 reauthorization extended benefits to underserved populations and prohibited requirements that sexual assault victims take polygraph tests before an investigation into their reports ensues. The 2012 renewal was also contentious, as conservatives opposed extending VAWA's provisions to same-sex couples.

The Great debate also surrounded extending the protections of VAWA to Native American women, as this brought up the typical jurisdictional battle that occurs with crime-related topics on tribal lands. Further, conservatives opposed extending VAWA's provisions to undocumented immigrant victims through the U Visa program. After expiring with the adjournment of the 112th Congress, VAWA was again reauthorized with all of the contentious provisions included in 2013.

The latest reauthorization was originally scheduled to occur by September 30 but has been extended to December 7 and December 21. It is temporarily reauthorized, but as of now, it appears politicians intend to block the reauthorization before the year's end, and out of 173 co-sponsors of the bill proposed by Representative Sheila Jackson Lee (D-Texas), none are Republicans. In all likelihood, the influx of women who were elected in the 2018 midterms in January 2019 would result in VAWA being reconsidered, but it is horrifying to see that once again there's even debate about supporting resources for victims. While no federal legislation is perfect, and VAWA can be legitimately critiqued for focusing too much on criminal justice and less on root causes of abuse, the 2018 reauthorization is still important. Jackson Lee's bill increases funding for sexual assault centers and expands the law related to removing guns from convicted abusers.

We should all implore Congress to act on the reauthorization of VAWA. As it becomes clearer that, according to a new study by the United Nations Office on Drugs and Crime, the least safe place for women globally is in the home, it is essential that our politicians take seriously the issues of domestic and sexual violence and not let political division disrupt these much-needed services.

68% of sexual assaults are not reported to police.
98% of rapists will never spend a day in jail or prison.

CHAPTER 7

RESISTANCE TACTICS

In a recent report by Erin Anderssen in October of 2018, a landmark Canadian study instructed participants on how to confront the risk of sexual assault on campus. While it's a partial solution – and an imperfect one – research shows resistance tactics work

In the debate over how to reduce sexual assault on university campuses, proposing self-defense classes for women is controversial. Women aren't the problem, the reasoning goes, so why is changing their behavior the solution? Putting the onus on women to drop-kick rapists, map out safe walks home, or geo-track their drinks at parties, writes the rules in the wrong direction. And it swerves too easily into victim-blaming.

But, according to new landmark Canadian research, it works. The study, published late 2018 in the New England Journal of Medicine, found that the Canadian-designed intervention, which focuses on teaching women how to detect risk in situations that could lead to sexual assault and defend themselves when necessary, reduced the rate of rape among participants by nearly 50 per cent. At a time when universities are facing harsh criticism for mishandling sexual assault, when the White House has called for action to reduce sexual violence on campus, when it's estimated that as many as one in four female university students may be assaulted before they finish their degree, is it responsible to deny young women access to a tried-and-tested program?

Lindsey Boyes, 22, took the course for extra credit in first-year psychology at the University of Calgary four years ago. She calls it a "paradigm shift" that corrected her own confusion about consent and lifted the guilt she felt about a sexual assault during her teen years. She describes the program as "useful and necessary for where we are now as a society." But, she says, "It's a Band-Aid. It doesn't get at the root of the problem."

The four-year study tracked nearly 900 women at three Canadian universities, randomly selecting half to take the 12-hour "resistance" program and compared them to a second group who received only brochures, similar to those available at a health clinic. One year later, the incidence of reported rape among women who took the program was 5.2 per cent, compared to 9.8 per cent in the control group; the gap in incidents of attempted rape was even wider.

The discomfiting part is that primarily the potential victims are still shouldering the burden for their own safety.

"There are no quick fixes," says lead author Charlene Senn, a women's studies professor at the University of Windsor. "We need multiple strategies. But we now know that giving women the right skills, and building the confidence that they can use them, does decrease their experience with sexual violence. This is our best short-term strategy while we wait for cultural change."

On the first of four Thursday evening sessions, Lindsey Boyes had to leave the room. She was shaking. The facilitator had just finished explaining how the Canadian Criminal Code says consent cannot be given when a person is incapacitated and intoxicated.

"It felt like she was talking directly to me," recalls Ms. Boyes, who joined the study for extra credit in her first-year psychology class at the University of Calgary.

When Ms. Boyes was 16, she'd gotten drunk at a party. An older boy – "the most popular guy" at her small-town school, she recalls – offered to help her find a place to sleep because her girlfriends had already left. She remembers throwing up, a lot, and then flashes of him on top of her in bed. "Afterwards, he said, 'Don't worry, I won't tell anybody.'" But word spread, and she went from being a virgin to a "slut" in one night. Even her friends told her, "You shouldn't have gotten so drunk." They were right, she decided, it was her fault.

Now, in this class, she was learning for the first time to see what happened as a crime for which she was not to blame. "It was pretty intense," recalls Ms. Boyes, now 22, who is going into her fourth year of a commerce degree. "It was a complete paradigm shift for me."

The prevention program is a modern step from those old-school, self-defense classes that suggested, misleadingly, that the biggest risks come from empty parking garages and strangers leaping from bushes. Participants are reminded in the first of four classes that at least 80 per cent of sexual assaults are perpetrated by someone the victim knows.

Eight hundred and ninety-three women were recruited mostly from first-year psychology classes at the Universities of Windsor, Calgary and Guelph. They ranged in age from 17 to 24. Half of them were living in residence. The women in the study were randomly selected into two comparable groups. Retention was high; about 90 per cent of women assigned to the intervention group completed at least three of the four session in the 12-hour program.

CONTROL GROUP		RESISTANCE GROUP
43.5%	POST-TEST — Forceful verbal strategies: yell, swear, scream in his face, etc.	56.5%
45.5%	1 YEAR LATER	54.5%
36.1%	POST-TEST — Forceful physical strategies: punch, hit, kick, bite, etc.	63.9%
37.6%	1 YEAR LATER	62.4%

Prior to taking the study, the rate of self-reported rape since age 14 in the entire group was 23 per cent, a number that may be higher than average because women with a history of sexual violence might have been more likely to volunteer for the study. But, at the same time, it's estimated that one in four university women will be sexual assaulted during their four years on campus. This figure is based largely on a Canadian study more than a decade old, and is the subject of some debate, but American research also suggests rates between 14 and 26 per cent.

In surveys, participants were asked to finish this sentence, "If a man I know, either a date or acquaintance, tried to force me to have sex with him, I would…." The group on the left is the control group; on the right, the women who received the intervention. These numbers show results one week after the intervention, and a year later. Women who took the program were more likely to say they would use force – the most effective strategy for stopping an assault.

The study tracked sexual assault among participants. The numbers above show actual counts of reported non-consensual sexual activity up to one year later. In all categories, the rates for the group receiving the intervention were consistently lower.

CONTROL GROUP		RESISTANCE GROUP
42	COMPLETED RAPE	23
40	ATTEMPTED RAPE	15
62	COERCION	48
103	ATTEMPTED COERCION	67
184	NONCONSENSUAL SEXUAL CONTACT	121

The rate of rape was reduced by half. Researchers believe this is because women learned to avoid risky situations and were more likely to stop coercive behavior before it escalated.

"The keys in the eyes are not going to work around your girlfriend's boyfriend," Prof. Senn likes to say. She cites studies that show women are the least likely to use force against acquaintances and friends, that perpetrators are more likely to lead with charm and alcohol than overt aggression. The course covers how to escape a choke hold, and ways to get out from underneath someone on a bed but focuses on how to prevent situations from going that far. The most powerful part of a woman's body, participants are told, is her voice. One of the central messages in the course: Don't worry about being polite. Trust your instincts.

"As women we are really taught not to offend, not to be rude to people," says Heidi Fischer, now 25, who participated in the study during her first year at the University of Guelph. "It's about getting in touch with your gut."

The course has four goals: to teach women common scenarios for sexual assault, how to recognize potential predators, how to evade danger (including through self-defense), and how to think about sexuality and relationships in terms of their own desires and boundaries.

Prof. Senn says the course stresses that learning skills does not mean women are to blame when an assault occurs; they also receive information on their rights, and how to file a complaint. (Ninety per cent of participants attended at least three of the three-hour sessions. Researchers offered small cash incentives, as is standard in trials, and guaranteed anonymity in the surveys. While researchers couldn't follow up on assaults, women were given material after completing surveys reminding them how to seek help.)

Natalie Hope, 22, took the course in her freshman year at the University of Guelph. "I realized there were so many times as a teenager that I was blind to what was going on," she says. "I really felt it was something I should have learned sooner." One take-home lesson: Don't disappear from your girlfriends; tell everyone where you are going. "We had a code phrase," Ms. Hope says. "If someone said, 'Oh, I like your shoes,' it meant 'I am uncomfortable, get me away.'" The course helped clarify her own comfort zone. Today, "I feel in control because I know what I expect."

The participants interviewed for this story could all give examples of ways they had used what they learned. They mentioned covering their drinks, being aware of their environment, speaking up sooner when a situation felt risky even if it meant offending someone. Six months after taking the course, Ms. Boyes was alone in a car with a first date, when he started to make her uncomfortable. "He was getting pretty pushy, and I told him to take me home," she says. "I am not sure I would have been that direct before."

"I pay more attention to what I am doing, how I am acting toward people," says Jenna Harris, 21, who is going into her fourth year at the University of Windsor. "I make sure I don't lead someone on," including accepting drinks from a stranger. She practices the buddy system at parties and bars, and she is more careful about her own alcohol consumption, because, she says, "if you are responsible for your friends, you are responsible for yourself as well."

While they called the material "empowering," and described sharing what they learned with friends, the women also said they felt conflicted. "It's keeping me safe, but it's not keeping everybody safe," Ms. Fischer says. "Why are we teaching women to be afraid, women to be cautious, instead of teaching men not to be perpetrators?"

Attacking the root, however, has proven more difficult. During frosh week at many North American universities, for instance, freshmen often receive a one- or two-hour workshop about consent. But according to a convincing stack of studies documented by the U.S. Centers for Disease Control and Prevention, this "education" has little to no influence on what happens during the alcohol-saturated parties that follow. Many programs were too short, the CDC concluded, to have any lasting impact, and tended to focus on areas such as legal implications, as if rape is caused "by a lack of awareness of the laws prohibiting it." Bystander programs which encourage male and female students to shut down sexist jokes or step in at parties when they see risky behavior have produced promising results, but cultural change, as Prof. Senn points out, is a long-term solution.

Many of the programs are offered too late – especially for young women like Lindsey Boyes. This was a common complaint among participants: Why hadn't they learned this when they were first exploring their sexuality, and short on confidence?

There is convincing evidence in the research for introducing these types of program much earlier. The CDC research found that the three interventions that proved most successful at reducing harassment and assaults were offered in middle school and high school – suggesting, researchers said, that these younger ages may represent a "critical window" to promote safer behavior.

But getting the program into schools can be challenging – as Ontario recently learned with the controversy around its new sex education curriculum, which includes information on consent. Prof. Senn had already faced that hurdle, when she offered the program to Windsor high schools; while the public board declined, she says, the Catholic board allowed the program provided she drop the final class on sexuality and relationships. Prof. Senn says the waiting lists to attend were so long they had to add extra sessions. Given that about half of the rape offenses women experience happen before they are 18, she says, "Adapting the program for girls in high school is a priority."

The program is not the full answer, researchers say, but it's an immediate real-world approach. "We shouldn't just sit around and wait for a cultural shift that isn't happening," says Lise Gotell, a women's study professor at the University of Alberta who is levelled at a women-centered approach. The larger lesson lies with the intervention's success. "When constraining women's actions is still the major way that we can respond to the threat of sexual assault," she says, "that is an indication of how much more we have to do."

The program will be familiar with the new Canadian study, and aware of the criticisms offered free to Canadian universities, though schools will have to cover the cost of facilitators, for whom training guidelines are now being developed. In an ideal world, says Prof. Senn, "this program would be available to all first-year women students until we don't need it any longer – that is, when sexual violence ends."

It's been a long road to get here from there. In writing this material I was personally astounded at the numbers within the data collected. The story is telling and poignant, yet it does not have to be the case.

Many of the reported cases could have been avoided or counterbalanced with personal information, self-security and safety measures as outlined in this text.

Not all could be prevented. There are far too many factors to include that are unreasonable to believe falsely that this horrible crime against women could be negated entirely, but some steps, few that are played out here could be the determining factor against you becoming one of the factors collected and assimilated within the data.

Don't be a number. Protect yourself at all times. It's a really big world out there and it is impossible to know everyone and everywhere. Take all the necessary steps for yourself to prevent an attack or assault. Rely on yourself for your own protection and feel confident in your own mind that you can protect yourself.

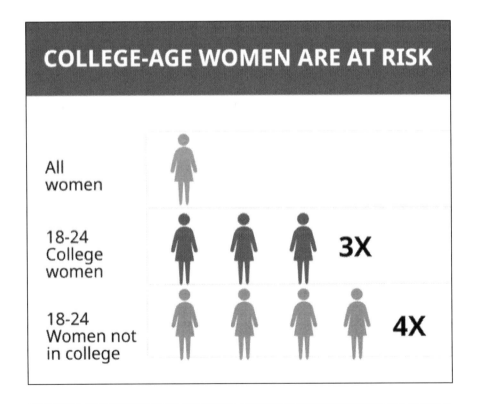

CHAPTER 8

REAL SELF DEFENSE TECHNIQUES

Taking a class once or twice will not develop a real self-defense attitude or ability. It will only give you a false sense of security and more than likely do more harm than good. If you take a class or course that is offered do not stop. Continue your practice and training and continue to learn and develop your self-defense skills to a mastery level. Only then will you have a real sense of safety and security. This can only come with practice and repetition of that practice. There is nothing in this manual that you can learn instantaneously and without practical application.

The techniques that I regularly teach my students and participants have been tested and work. In real combat, things change and there is a myriad of variables. Learning and practicing on those variables are what can truly protect you.

The techniques that are shown in this material are techniques that potentially can save your life or protect you if attacked. However, because these are techniques in a book you should always find a hands-on instructor to learn from. The techniques in this material are for your own selection to choose from to practice. Practice one or practice them all, remember that if done correctly with proper timing and diligent practice will you be able to defend yourself in a given situation.

There are no guarantees in life nor in training for protection. There is only the practice and of being more aware and able to move in a state of self-awareness that makes it the determining factor in an assault or attack upon your person.

Practice, practice, practice. That is the only thing that helps you learn and develop those needed skills for anything in life.

We do as we train to do! If possible, find a partner and study slowly the movements and techniques listed herein. It's great to be able to just jump in at full speed and do the steps but it may lead to injury to yourself and give you a misrepresentation of what may actually happen.

Becoming empowered leads you to become more aware of your surroundings and your own security.

With that in mind let's begin the training tips. Good luck and keep focused.

Here are a few scenarios that can occur during an attack. These are simple techniques that can help prevent you from bodily harm or worse. These simplified defenses are easy to perform and can cause bodily harm. Please practice with caution.

REAR CHOKE/ GRAB DEFENSES

REAL SELF DEFENSE FOR WOMEN

As the attacker reaches around for a single arm choke. The defender should always be aware of their surroundings and be prepared for anything. By raising the hands up and between you and the choker, this eliminates the possibility of being choked out or passing out during an attack.

REAL SELF DEFENSE FOR WOMEN

Allowing an attacker to grab around the neck area can be lethal.

REAL SELF DEFENSE FOR WOMEN

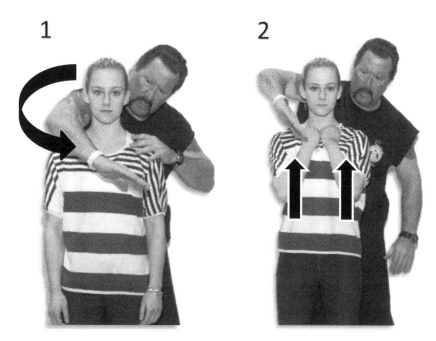

The defender raises both hands straight up to their chin. This can help prevent a choking situation where the defender cannot breathe.

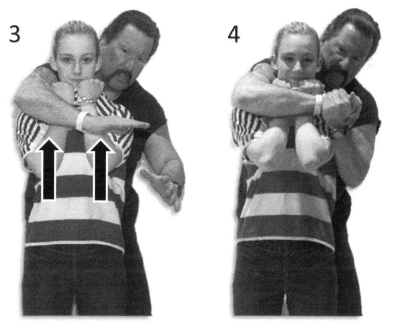

1-4. Raising your hands to your chin and under the arms of the attacker during this type of attack prevents the attacker from choking.

REAL SELF DEFENSE FOR WOMEN

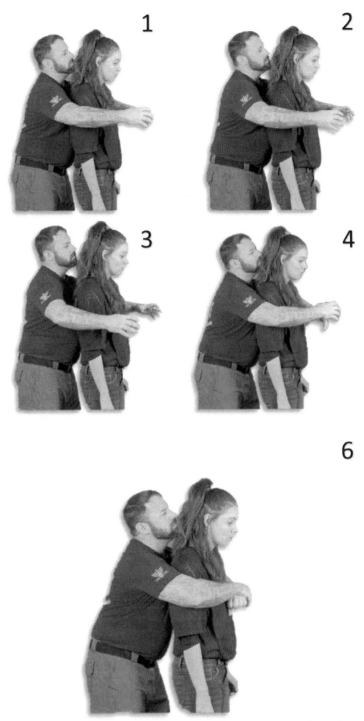

1-6. Attacker from behind grabs and lifts with both arms / hands.

REAL SELF DEFENSE FOR WOMEN

7-12. attacker lifts defender from ground- Defender kicks with heel or flat of foot in to attackers mid quadricep muscle or front of leg.

REAL SELF DEFENSE FOR WOMEN

13. (Close-Up) Kicking attacker in mid leg or quadricep. Use the heel for maximum impact and damage.

14

Simultaneously defender can whip their head backwards to strike attackers face / head to cause severe injury to attacker. (Close-up) Striking attackers face or head.

REAL SELF DEFENSE FOR WOMEN

15

16

15-16 Once the defender has made the head strike the defender can then use their body weight to break the attackers grip. By throwing the weight forward using the head a, legs and body the defender can easily out maneuver the attacker's grip.

REAL SELF DEFENSE FOR WOMEN

17

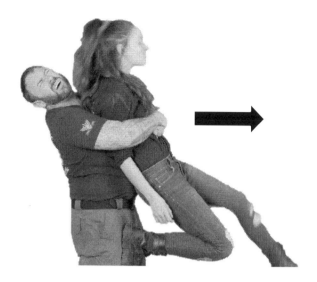

18

17-18. After smashing the back of the head into the attacker's face, use the momentum forward and push off and away against the attacker's body.

REAL SELF DEFENSE FOR WOMEN

19-20. Falling forward using the momentum of the push against the attacker, throw yourself forward creating too much pressure on the attacker's grasp / hold. Fall forward and once the attacker releases his grip run away and find help in a public place or call police.

REAL SELF DEFENSE FOR WOMEN

1-4. The attacker grabs around from behind attempting to hold / control the defender.

REAL SELF DEFENSE FOR WOMEN

5

5. Defender uses the elbow to strike backwards in to the attacker's body. Ribcage, side of body, chest are all sensitive areas.

6

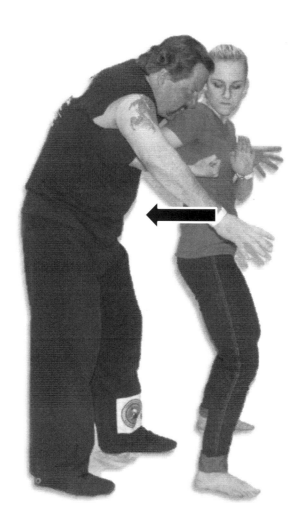

6. Defender smashes elbow in to the attacker's body.

REAL SELF DEFENSE FOR WOMEN

7

7. Once free defender should run away.

DO NOT STAY AND FIGHT. RUN AWAY

REAL SELF DEFENSE FOR WOMEN

1-4. Attacker attempts to grab hold from behind.

REAL SELF DEFENSE FOR WOMEN

5. Defender uses the elbow to strike vital areas of the attacker's body. Thrusting the elbow backwards toward the attacker's body.

6

6. Defender strikes the elbow upward toward the jaw / face of attacker.

7

7. The defender strikes hard to the jaw / face of attacker.

8. Striking the Face / Jaw of attacker upwards can cause serious injury. The attacker can easily bite down on his tongue or inside the cheek. The strike may also move upwards toward the nose fracturing / breaking the nose bone / cartilage.

REAL SELF DEFENSE FOR WOMEN

9

9. The defender runs away. Go directly to police or seek help in a public place when possible.

DO NOT STAY AND FIGHT RUN AWAY

REAL SELF DEFENSE FOR WOMEN

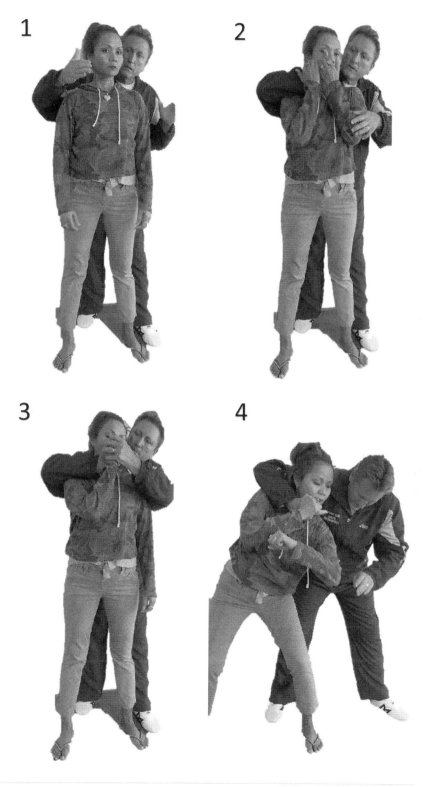

1-6. The attacker reaches around from behind and grabs / chokes the defender. The defender steps slightly aside and strikes backwards and down toward the groin of the attacker. Once free Run Away.

REAL SELF DEFENSE FOR WOMEN

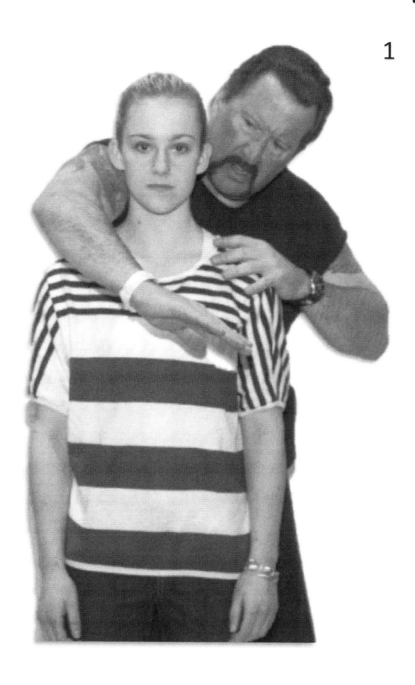

1

1. Attacker reaches around from behind to choke / hold defender.

REAL SELF DEFENSE FOR WOMEN

2

2. As the attacker reaches around the neck, an alternative to raising your hands to neck level is by simply turning your head toward the inside of the attacker's arm. This is a good prevention as well from a choke assualt.

REAL SELF DEFENSE FOR WOMEN

3

As the attacker reaches around, Defender grabs fingers / Fingertips of the attacker. (Close-Up) grabbing the fingers of the attacker firmly.

REAL SELF DEFENSE FOR WOMEN

4

Pushing up on the outside of the elbow of the attacker and pulling fingertips outward and away from your body allows space to move out of the choke hold position.

REAL SELF DEFENSE FOR WOMEN

5. Pushing up/ lifting on the outside of the elbow of the attacker and pulling fingertips outward away from your body allows space to move out of the choke hold position.

REAL SELF DEFENSE FOR WOMEN

6. Pushing outward and away on the attacker's elbow while pulling back and down on the attackers fingers / Hand. Allows the defender to push the assailant away without much force.

Push away and run.

DO NOT STAY AND FIGHT.

FRONT SINGLE HAND ATTACK/GRAB DEFENSES

REAL SELF DEFENSE FOR WOMEN

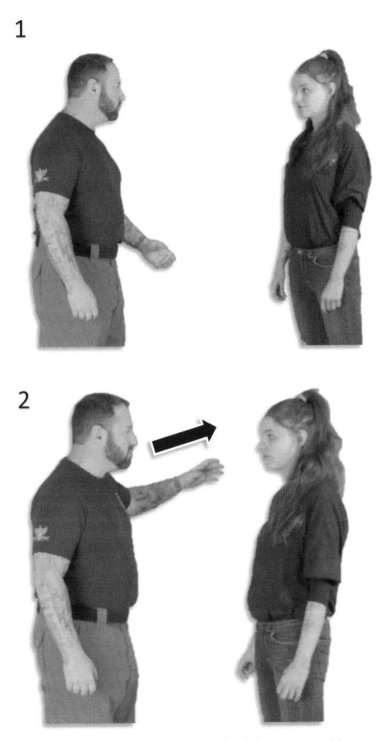

1-2. Attacker reaches outward to grab the defender's shoulder

REAL SELF DEFENSE FOR WOMEN

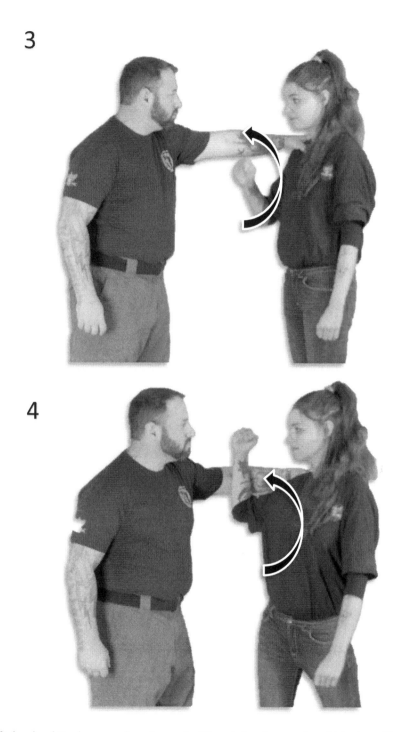

3-4. As Attacker reaches to grab- The defender parries / blocks with an upward circular block to the attacker's arm.

REAL SELF DEFENSE FOR WOMEN

5. (Close-up) A circular block to the attacker's arm can easily take aggressors arm away from the shoulder.

REAL SELF DEFENSE FOR WOMEN

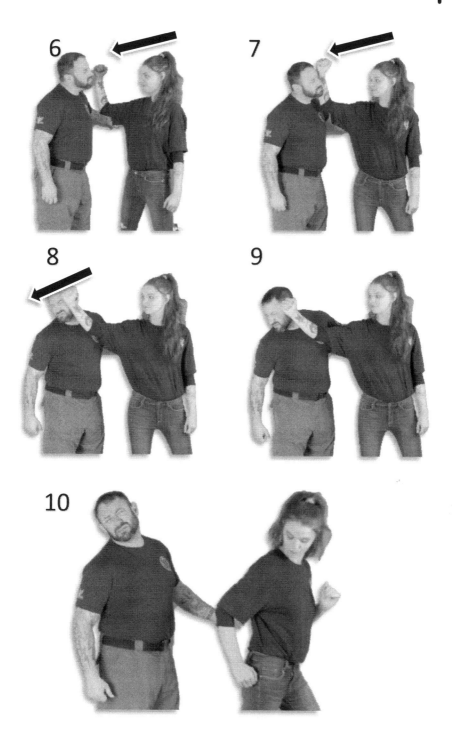

6-10. Using the same arm that blocked the defender can now strike the face/head of attacker and turn to run away.

REAL SELF DEFENSE FOR WOMEN

1-4. The attacker grabs / holds the wrist / lower arm of defender. The defender steps away from the attacker gaining space. The defender kicks low to the attacker's knee. This can cause serious injury to the attacker.

REAL SELF DEFENSE FOR WOMEN

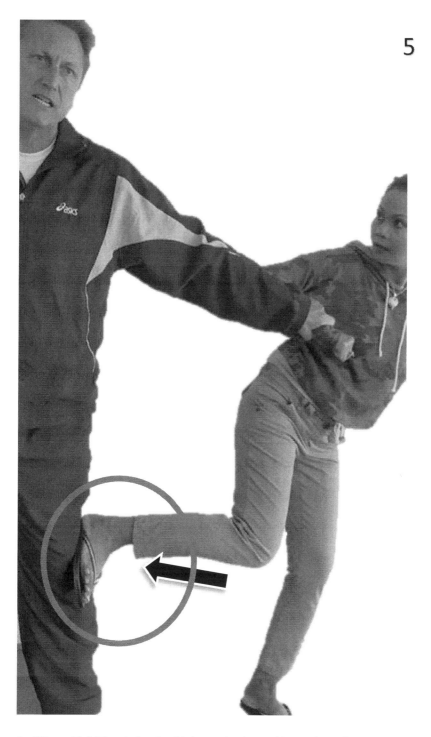

5. (Close-Up) The defender kicks at the knee / lower leg of attacker causing severe damage and pain. Once free Run Away.

REAL SELF DEFENSE FOR WOMEN

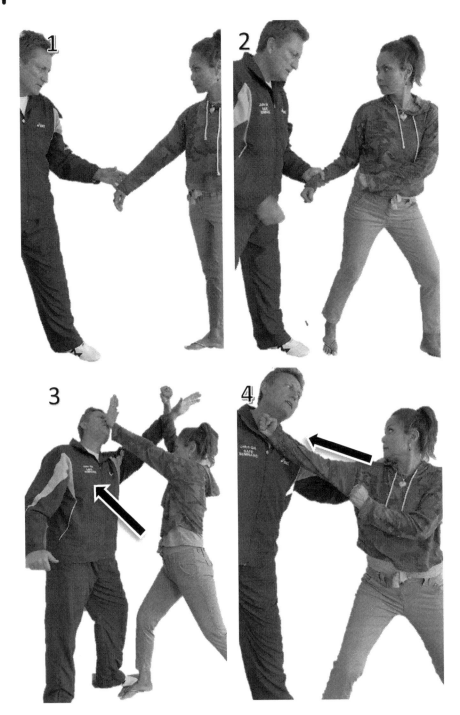

1-4. The attacker grabs / holds the wrist / lower arm of the defender. The defender moves forward toward the attacker. Raising both hands upward.one hand free can strike to the face of the attacker as the other releases the grip from the attacker's grasp.

REAL SELF DEFENSE FOR WOMEN

5

5. Using the elbow the defender can continue their defense stepping in toward the attacker with an elbow strike to the face / neck of the attacker.

1

1. The attacker grabs the wrist or lower arm of defender.

REAL SELF DEFENSE FOR WOMEN

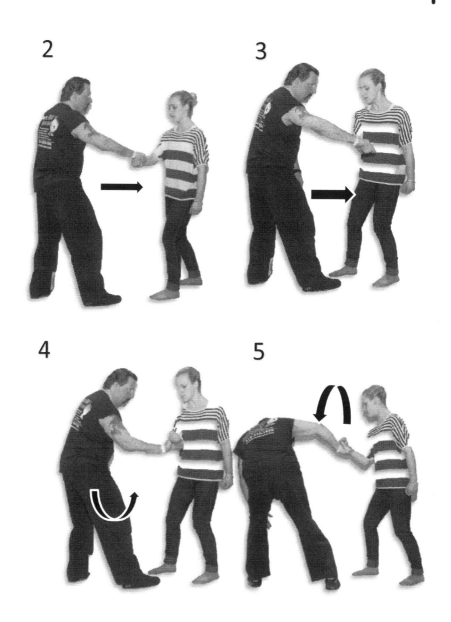

2-5. The defender pulls slightly inward and with a circular motion turns the hand upwards and over.

REAL SELF DEFENSE FOR WOMEN

6

6. The defender can strike the upper ribs or side of attacker hard. Then run away.

DO NOT STAY AND FIGHT

REAL SELF DEFENSE FOR WOMEN

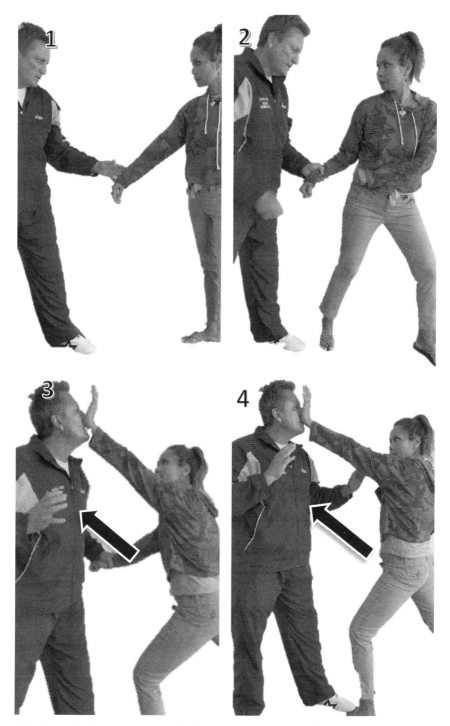

1-4. the attacker grabs / holds the wrist / lower arm of the defender. The defender steps toward the attacker with the free hand smashing the attacker in the face / nose with a palm / hand strike.

REAL SELF DEFENSE FOR WOMEN

5. The defender strikes to the jaw / face of attacker. This may cause a fracture of the nose cartilage / cheek bones or jaw of the attacker. Please caution when practicing this technique.

6

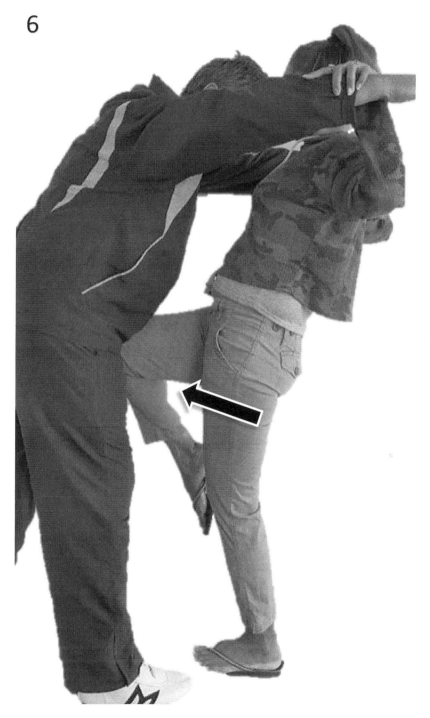

6. The defense can continue with a knee strike in to the groin or abdomen of the attacker to finish off the attacker's aggression.

FRONT DOUBLE HAND ATTACK/GRAB DEFENSES

REAL SELF DEFENSE FOR WOMEN

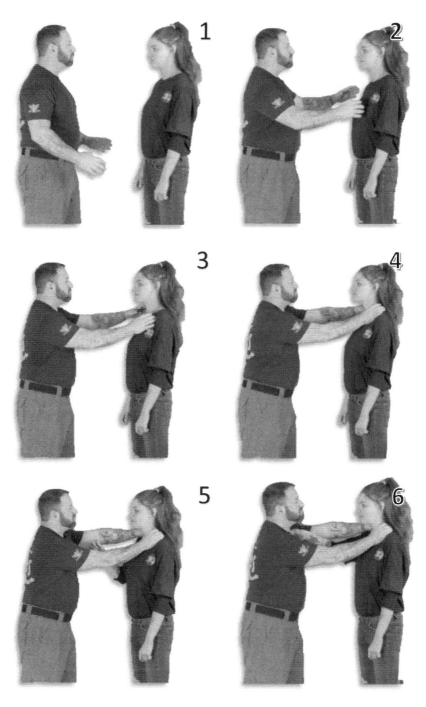

1-6. Attacker grabs/ Chokes with both hands. As attacker grabs / chokes Defender only uses the thumb/ thumbnail to strike the throat or Adams apple of attacker.

REAL SELF DEFENSE FOR WOMEN

7. (Close-up) Defender strikes the throat or Adams apple of attacker. Defender should immediately run away and seek help

REAL SELF DEFENSE FOR WOMEN

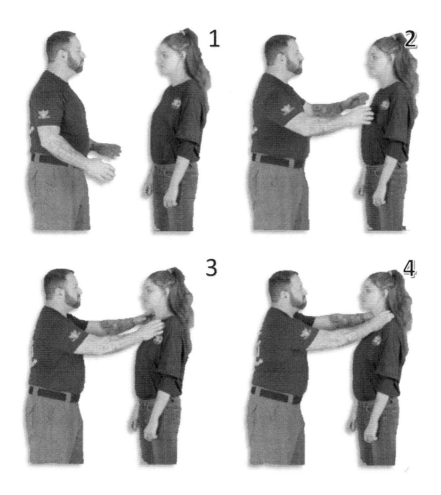

1-4. The attacker reaches toward the defender with both hands. This can be either a shoulder grab or a choking assualt.

This is a common attack against women and can be very violent.

REAL SELF DEFENSE FOR WOMEN

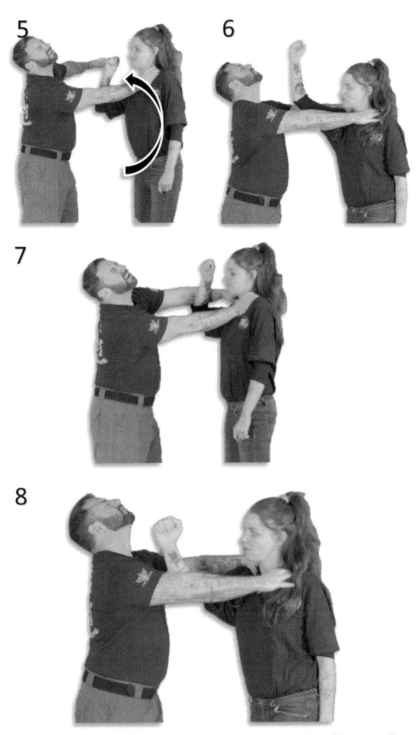

5-8. The defender uses the same circular motion mentioned in a previous defense. Striking the inside of the arm of the attacker.

9

9. (Close-Up) In the close up the defender can be seen striking / blocking the attacker's arm from the inside. Hitting inside the forearm near the middle of the forearm for the best results.

10

11

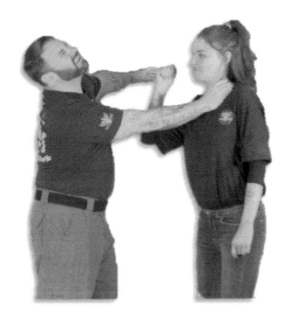

10-11. Carrying the motion through the defender can choose to strike the face or head of the attacker or continue through and strike the remaining arm on the opposite side of the body.

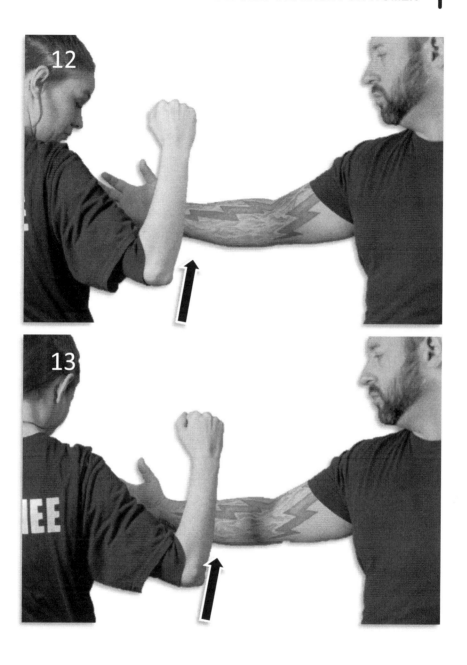

12-13. Using a continuous motion follow through with the striking hand across the body striking the attackers other arm.

REAL SELF DEFENSE FOR WOMEN

14

14. (Close-Up) the defender should strike in the soft tissue area of the middle of the inside of the forearm of the attacker for maximum results.

15

16

15-16. Once the remaining arm has fallen away the defender should turn and run away.

DO NOT STAY AND FIGHT.

REAL SELF DEFENSE FOR WOMEN

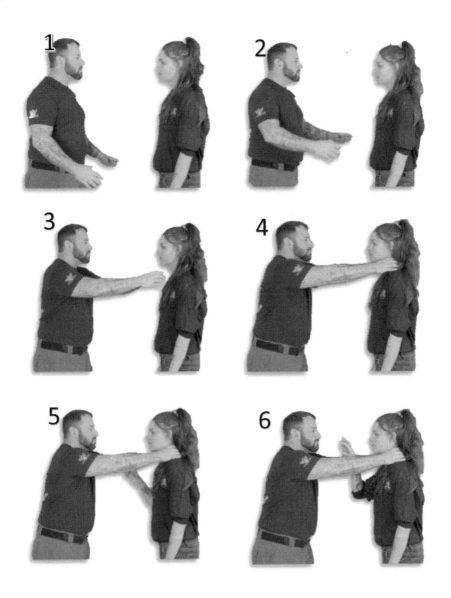

1-6. Attacker grabs/ chokes with both hands. The defender strikes forward into the eyes and/ or face of attacker.

REAL SELF DEFENSE FOR WOMEN

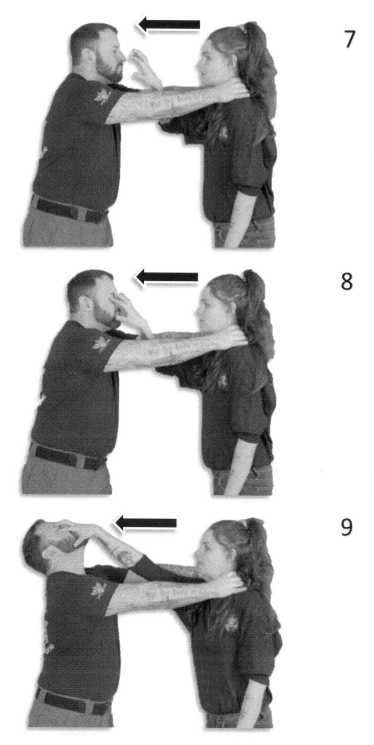

7-9. The defender lunges the hand forward with fingers outstretched striking the vital and sensitive areas in the face.

10

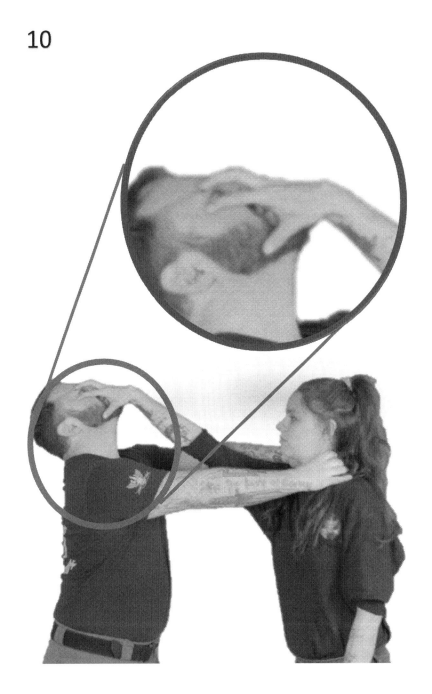

10. (Close-Up) the fingers can easily reach the soft vital areas of the face including the eyes, nose or sinuses and scratch the surface of the face and skin harshly, causing severe pain to attacker.

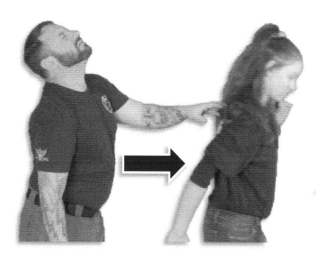

11-12. Simply turning away from the attacker and run away is the best solution. Seek help from Police or nearby business.

FRONT ATTACK/GRAB DAILY ITEM DEFENSES

REAL SELF DEFENSE FOR WOMEN

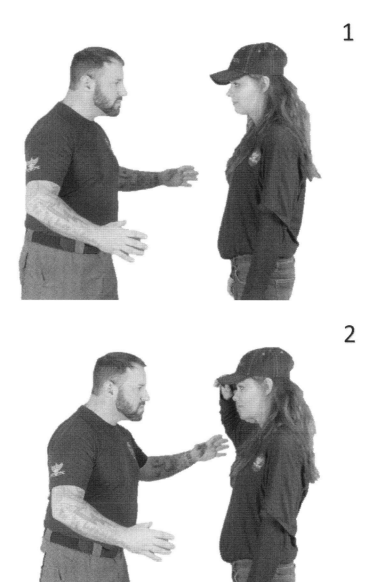

1-2. The attacker lunges forward with either hand to strike / push / grab the defender

REAL SELF DEFENSE FOR WOMEN

3

4

3-4. The defender grabs the hat and with force swings the hat at the attacker's face.

REAL SELF DEFENSE FOR WOMEN

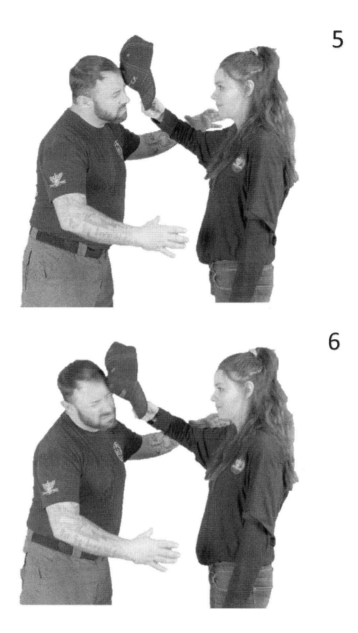

5-6. The hat will strike the face, eyes, nose and soft tissue areas of the face causing tremendous pain to the attacker.

REAL SELF DEFENSE FOR WOMEN

7

8

7-8. Continued motion, Swing through the strike at attacker's face and head area for maximum result.

REAL SELF DEFENSE FOR WOMEN

9

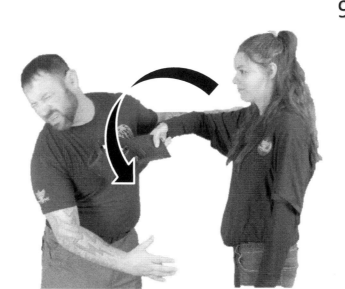

10

9-10. With full force aim for the face and soft tissue areas of the head of the attacker. Then turn and run away

DO NOT STAY AND FIGHT

Seek Police or help quickly in a public place.

REAL SELF DEFENSE FOR WOMEN

1-6. Attacker reaches out to grab / hold / choke defender.

REAL SELF DEFENSE FOR WOMEN

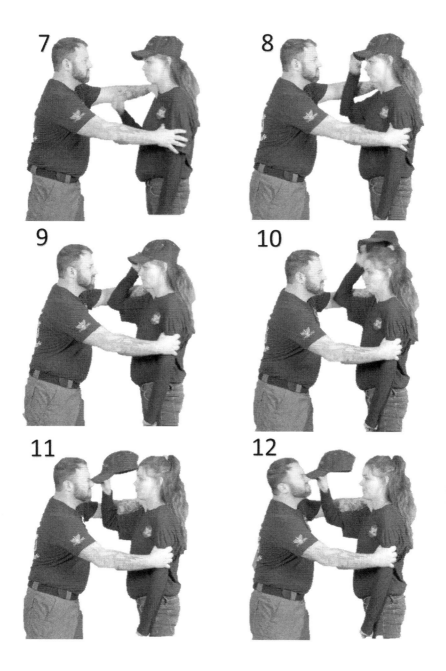

7-12. As attacker reaches to grab the defender easily grabs the brim of the ballcap / baseball hat firmly. Pushing the edge of the brim outward and striking in to the arch of the attacker's nose.

REAL SELF DEFENSE FOR WOMEN

13. (Close-Up) Striking the bridge of the nose can fracture the cartilage in the nose.

REAL SELF DEFENSE FOR WOMEN

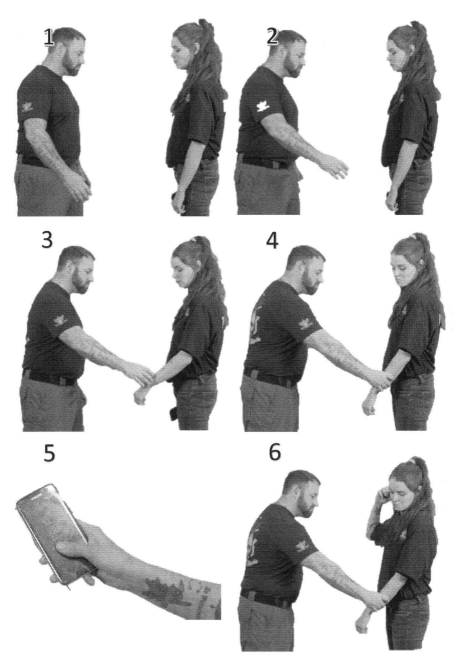

1-6. The attacker reaches out to grab / hold the defender by the wrist or lower arm. The defender uses her cell phone with a firm grip. Strike downward toward the attacker's mid forearm or wrist.

REAL SELF DEFENSE FOR WOMEN

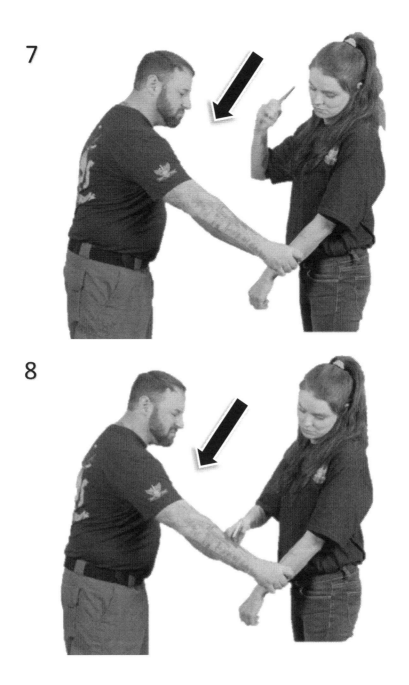

7-8. Striking downward the defender uses the phone as a weapon to strike the attacker's arm / mid forearm.

REAL SELF DEFENSE FOR WOMEN

9. (Close-Up) The defender uses the cell phone to strike the mid forearm of the attacker. With enough force it is possible to break r fracture the forearm using a cell phone.

REAL SELF DEFENSE FOR WOMEN

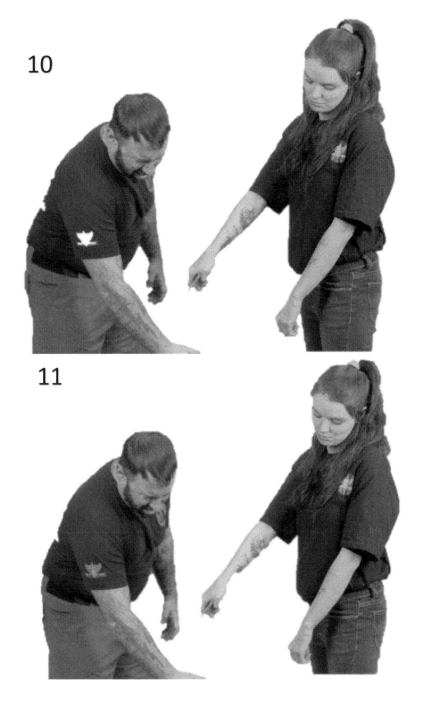

10-11. Once the grasp of the attacker is loosened the defender should turn and run. Seek help from Police or others in a public area.

REAL SELF DEFENSE FOR WOMEN

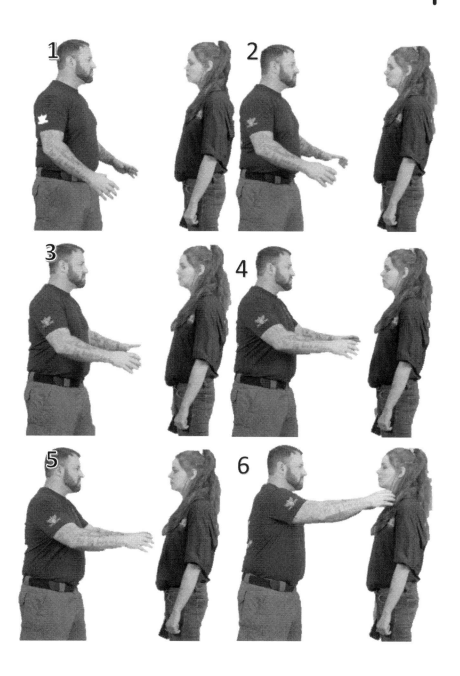

1-6. The attacker reaches with both hands to choke/ strangle/ hold the defender.

REAL SELF DEFENSE FOR WOMEN

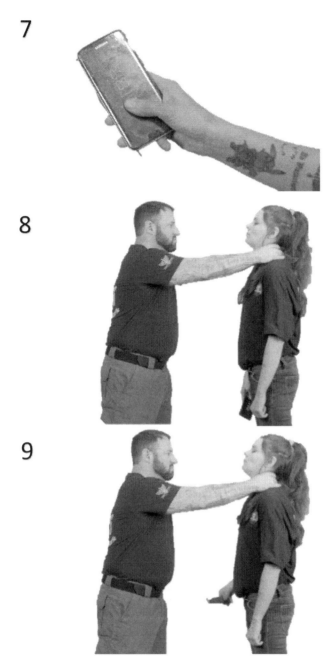

7-9. Gripping the cell phone firmly it can be used as a weapon to defend against attacks.

REAL SELF DEFENSE FOR WOMEN

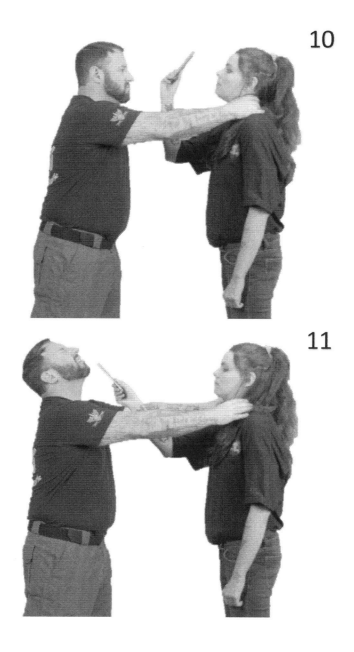

10-11. The defender using the cell phone firmly in hand strikes at the face nose / head of the attacker.

REAL SELF DEFENSE FOR WOMEN

12-13. (Close-Up) Striking the soft tissues and vulnerable areas such as the nose/ face/ head of the attacker with a normal cell phone can cause serious damage to any attacker.

REAL SELF DEFENSE FOR WOMEN

1

2

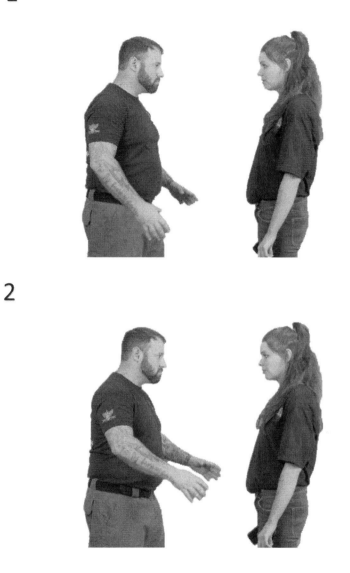

1-2. The attacker reaches out to grab / hold   choke the defender.

REAL SELF DEFENSE FOR WOMEN

3

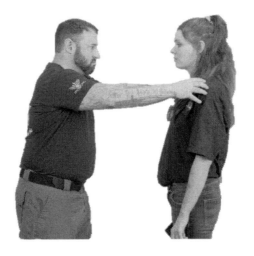

4

3-4. As the attacker grasp the defender the defender firmly grips the cell phone in hand.

REAL SELF DEFENSE FOR WOMEN

5

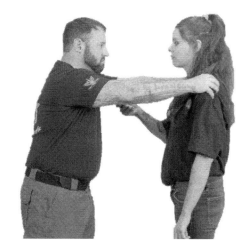

6

5-6. The defender thrust the cell phone toward the attacker.

7

8

7-8. The defender strikes the attacker in the throat. Cutting off air and blood circulation to the attacker.

REAL SELF DEFENSE FOR WOMEN

9

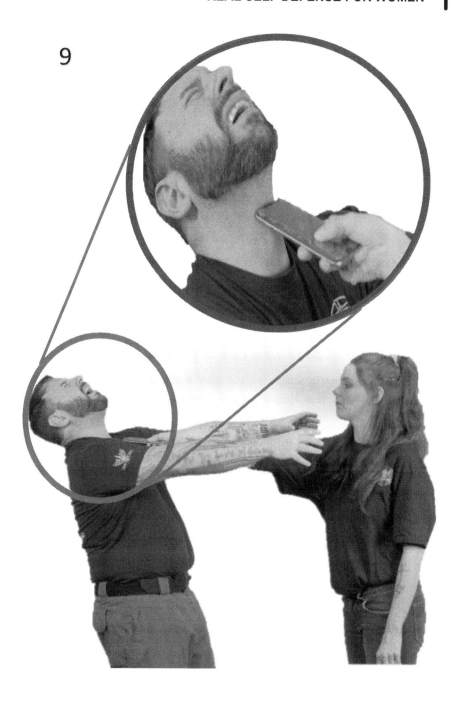

9. Thrusting the phone forward into the attacker's throat can cause serious injury and possible death. Be cautious when practicing this technique. It can cause serious injury during practice.

CHAPTER 9

THE CALL FOR HELP

Crime-Statistics Against Women

The crime-statistics show that about 31 million total crimes are reported in the United States annually. That's about one crime per second.

Victim rates of violent crimes have increased. Without warning, a situation can turn from safe to sorry; turning you not only into a victim, but the top news story of the day.

And, most people who are victimized never imagined that crime would happen to them. *It always happens to the other person.*

The crime-statistics indicate that in the next hour, somewhere in the United States, the following will happen:

- 900 Thefts
- 189 Violent Crimes
- 124 Assaults
- 66 Robberies
- 24 Sexual Assaults
- 12 Rapes
- 2 Murders

REAL SELF DEFENSE FOR WOMEN

Statistical Overview of Crime & Victimization in the United States

- 47% of violent crimes and 40% of property crime was reported to the police.
- An estimated 16,692 persons were murdered nationwide in 2005; an increase of 3.4% from the 2004 figure.
- In 2005, 389,100 women and 78,180 men were victimized by an intimate partner.
- In 2005, victims experienced 191,670 incidents of rape and sexual assault.
- More than one million women and almost 400,000 men are stalked annually in the United States.
- In 2005, teens ages 12 to 19 and young adults ages 20 to 24 experienced the highest rates of violent crime.
- In 2005, teenagers (ages 12 to 19) experienced 1.5 million violent crimes; this figure includes 176,020 robberies and 73,470 sexual assaults and rapes.
- In 2005, 24% of all violent crime incidents were committed by an armed offender, and 9% by an offender with a firearm.
- An average of 1.7 million people are victims of violent crime while working or on duty each year. An estimated 1.3 million (75%) of these incidents are simple assaults while an additional 19% are aggravated assaults.
- In 2005, 95,426 crimes were reported on college and university campuses; 97% were property crimes and 3% were violent crimes.

REAL SELF DEFENSE FOR WOMEN

Homicide Statistics

- The crime-statistics show that of female murder victims in 2005, 33.4% were killed by their husbands or boyfriends. In contrast, 2.4% of the male victims were murdered by their wives or girlfriends.
- In 2005, homicides occurred in connection with another felony (such as rape, robbery or arson) in 23% of incidents.

5 major cities with the most murders in 2017

● 2017   ○ 2016

Chicago: 650 / 762
Baltimore: 343 / 318
Philadelphia: 317 / 277
New York: 290 / 335
Los Angeles: 286 / 293

SOURCE USA TODAY analysis of police department crime data

Campus Crime Statistics

- In 2005, 189,448 crimes were reported on college and university campuses; 97% were property crimes and 3% were violent crimes.
- Crime-statistics indicate that of the violent crimes reported on college campuses, 1,445 (53%) were aggravated assaults, 761 (28%) were robberies, 1,000 (18%) were forcible rapes, and 5 (01.%) were murders.
- In 2001, more than 97,000 students between the ages of 18 and 24 were victims of alcohol-related sexual assault or date rape. More than 696,000 students between the ages of 18 and 24 were assaulted by another student who had been drinking.
- 13% of college women were stalked at some point between the fall of 1996 and spring of 1997. Four in five campus stalking victims knew their attackers; and three in ten college women reported being injured emotionally or psychologically from being stalked.
- White college students had higher rates of violent victimization than students of other races.
- Victims of sexual assault were about four times more likely to be victimized by someone they knew than by a stranger.
- 9% of violent victimizations involved offenders armed with firearms; 7% were committed with knives; and 10% were committed with other types of weapons, such as a blunt object.
- **About 35% of violent victimizations against college students were reported to the police.**

- Most crimes against students (93%) occurred off campus; 72% of those crimes occurred at night.
- In 2003, crimes occurring in on-campus residence halls included 955 assaults, 1,808 forcible sex offenses, and 24 non-forcible sex offenses.

REAL SELF DEFENSE FOR WOMEN

Domestic Violence/Intimate Partner Violence Statistics

- In 2005, 389,100 women and 78,180 men were victimized by an intimate partner. These crimes accounted for 9% of all violent crime.
- The crime-statistics of female murder victims indicates that 33.4% were killed by their husbands or boyfriends; 2.4% of male murder victims were killed by their wives or girlfriends.
- 3% of all murders committed in the workplace were committed by the victim's intimate partner (either husband, wife or boyfriend).

- Domestic violence victims constituted 25% of all adult victims compensated by victim compensation programs in 2004. They received compensation for 34% of all assault claims.
- One study found that women who have experienced any type of personal violence (even when the last episode was 14 to 30 years ago) reported a greater number of chronic physical symptoms than those who have not been abused. The risk of suffering from six or more chronic physical symptoms increased with the number of forms of violence experienced.
- **Approximately 1 in 5 high school girls reported being abused by a boyfriend.**

Workplace Violence Statistics

- The crime-statistics for each year between 1993 and 1999, an average of 1.7 million people were victims of violent crime while working or on duty. An estimated 75% of these incidents were simple assaults, while an additional 19% were aggravated assaults.
- An average of 1.3 million simple assaults, 325,000 aggravated assaults, 70,100 robberies, 36,500 rapes and sexual assaults and 900 homicides occur in the United States each year.
- Nearly 80% of workplace homicides are committed by criminals otherwise unconnected to the workplace.
- Women are victims of 80% of rapes or sexual assaults in the workplace.
- 12% of workplace violence victims sustain injuries. More than half of these victims are not treated or do not receive medical treatment.
- Crime-statistics indicate that homicide accounts for 40% of all workplace deaths among female workers.
- Female workers are also at risk for nonfatal violence. Women were the victims in nearly two-thirds of the injuries resulting from workplace assaults. Most of these assaults (70%) were directed at women employed in service organizations, such as health care, while an additional 20% of these incidents occurred in retail locations, such as restaurants and grocery stores.

REAL SELF DEFENSE FOR WOMEN

Do you have the necessary knowledge and skill set to protect yourself against one of these crimes and not be counted in the next crime-statistics? Do you know what to do if confronted by an attacker? Do you have a game plan to deal with violent crime?

Family and domestic violence is a leading cause of homelessness:

72,000 women   **34,000 children**   **9,000 men**

sought homelessness services due to family violence in 2016–17

Intimate partner violence is the greatest health risk factor for women

aged **25–44**

$22 billion

was the estimated cost of violence against women and children in Australia in 2015–16

While preventing and responding to violence against women requires a multi-sectoral approach, the health sector has an important role to play. The health sector can:

- Advocate to make violence against women unacceptable and for such violence to be addressed as a public health problem.

- Provide comprehensive services, sensitize and train health care providers in responding to the needs of survivors holistically and empathetically.

- Prevent recurrence of violence through early identification of women and children who are experiencing violence and providing appropriate referral and support

- Promote egalitarian gender norms as part of life skills and comprehensive sexuality education curricula taught to young people.

- Generate evidence on what works and on the magnitude of the problem by carrying out population-based surveys or including violence against women in population-based demographic and health surveys, as well as in surveillance and health information systems.

In the majority of countries with available data, less than 40 per cent of the women who experience violence seek help of any sort. Among women who do, most look to family and friends and very few look to formal institutions and mechanisms, such as police and health services. Less than 10 per cent of those women seeking help for experience of violence sought help by appealing to the police.

At least 144 countries have passed laws on domestic violence, and 154 have laws on sexual harassment. However, even when laws exist, this does not mean they are always compliant with international standards and recommendations or implemented.

Availability of data on violence against women has increased significantly in recent years. Since 1995, more than 100 countries have conducted at least one survey addressing the issue. More than 40 countries conducted at least two surveys in the period between 1995 and 2014, which means that, depending on the comparability of the surveys, changes over time could be analyzed.

In an evaluation of 12 support groups for women victims of domestic assault revealed substantial benefits associated with group participation. A total of 76 women responded to an assessment package before, immediately after, and six months following the group. Significant improvements were found in self-esteem, belonging support, focus of control, less traditional attitudes towards marriage and the family, perceived stress, and marital functioning. Unexpectedly, clients currently living with their spouses also reported significant decreases in both physical and nonphysical abuse.

There are many support groups throughout the world for the safety and protection of women. Considering the number of groups reviewed. The most common program objectives included: To ensure the victims' safety, including the development of a safety plan in case the member should be placed in further jeopardy by her partner; ▯ To bring about an end to the physical violence as well as other forms of abusive behavior including verbal denigration, and sexual coercion; To educate members regarding the problem of wife assault such as prevalence, etiology and the cyclical nature of violence; To provide a supportive environment; create an atmosphere where clients can feel free to help one another; To increase members' sense of self-worth and in doing so to empower them so that they will not return to their previous sense of helplessness; To help members express extremely intense affect, especially anger, and to learn improved methods of emotional expression; To assist clients in identifying and understanding stereotyped attitudes and to explore their own personal relationships with an eye towards power and control issues which are reinforced in our society.

If you or someone you may know needs assistance or direct help feel free to contact the National Sexual Assault Telephone Hotline

Call 800.656.HOPE (4673) to be connected with a trained staff member from a sexual assault service provider in your area.

When you call 800.656.HOPE (4673), you'll be routed to a local RAINN affiliate organization based on the first six digits of your phone number. Cell phone callers have the option to enter the ZIP code of their current location to more accurately locate the nearest sexual assault service provider.

REAL SELF DEFENSE FOR WOMEN

Telephone Hotline Terms of Service

Calling the National Sexual Assault Hotline gives you access to a range of free services including:

- Confidential support from a trained staff member
- Support finding a local health facility that is trained to care for survivors of sexual assault and offers services like sexual assault forensic exams
- Someone to help you talk through what happened
- Local resources that can assist with your next steps toward healing and recovery
- Referrals for long term support in your area
- Information about the laws in your community
- Basic information about medical concerns

The National Sexual Assault Hotline is a safe, confidential service. When you call the hotline, only the first six numbers of the phone number are used to route the call, and your complete phone number is never stored in our system. Most states do have laws that require local staff to contact authorities in certain situations, like if there is a child or vulnerable adult who is in danger.

While almost all callers are connected directly to a staff member or volunteer at a local sexual assault service provider, a handful of providers use an answering service after daytime business hours. This service helps manage the flow of calls. If all staff members are busy, you may choose to leave a phone number with the answering service. In this case, the number will be confidential and will be given directly to the organization's staff member for a callback. If you reach an answering service, you can try calling back after some time has passed, or you can choose to call during regular business hours when more staff members are available.

Sexual assault service providers are organizations or agencies dedicated to supporting survivors of sexual assault. The providers who answer calls placed to the hotline are known as RAINN affiliates. To be part of the National Sexual Assault Hotline, affiliates must agree to uphold RAINN's confidentiality standards. That means:

- Never releasing records or information about the call without the consent of the caller, except when obligated by law
- Only making reports to the police or other agencies when the caller consents, unless obligated by law
- Agreeing to RAINN's non-discrimination policy

To learn more about how a provider can become an affiliate of the National Sexual Assault Hotline, visit the Sexual Assault Service Provider information page or email valeriet@rainn.org. Volunteer opportunities for the National Sexual Assault Hotline are coordinated through these local providers. **Search for volunteer opportunities** near you.

The National Sexual Assault Hotline was the nation's first decentralized hotline, connecting those in need with help in their local communities. It's made up of a network of independent sexual assault service providers, vetted by RAINN, who answer calls to a single, nationwide hotline number. Since it was first created in 1994, the National Sexual Assault Hotline (800.656.HOPE and **online.rainn.org**) has helped more than 2 million people affected by sexual violence.

Before the telephone hotline was created, there was no central place where survivors could get help. Local sexual assault services providers were well equipped to handle support services, but the lack of a national hotline meant the issue did not receive as much attention as it should. In response, RAINN developed a unique national hotline system to combine all the advantages of a national organization with all the abilities and expertise of local programs. One nationwide hotline number makes it easier for survivors to be connected with the help they deserve.

Anyone affected by sexual assault, whether it happened to you or someone you care about, can find support on the National Sexual Assault Hotline. You can also visit **online.rainn.org** to receive support via confidential online chat.

At the National Domestic Violence Hotline, highly trained expert advocates are available 24/7 to talk confidentially with anyone in the United States who is experiencing domestic violence, seeking resources or information, or questioning unhealthy aspects of their relationship.

The Hotline provides lifesaving tools and immediate support to empower victims and survivors to find safety and live free of abuse. We also provide support to friends and family members who are concerned about a loved one. Resources and help can be found by calling 1-800-799-SAFE (7233). Individuals who are

Deaf or hard of hearing may use TTY 1-800-787-3224. Additionally, advocates who are Deaf are available 24/7 through the National Deaf Hotline by video phone at 1-855-812-1001, Instant Messenger (Deaf Hotline) or email (nationaldeafhotline@adwas.org).

If it's not safe for you to call, or if you don't feel comfortable doing so, another option for getting direct help is to use our live chat service here on this website. You'll receive the same one-on-one, real-time, confidential support from a trained advocate as you would on the phone. Chat is available every day from 24/7/365. El chat en español está disponible de 12 p.m. - 6 p.m. Hora Central.

NUMBER OF PEOPLE VICTIMIZED EACH YEAR

Inmates:
80,600 were sexually assaulted or raped[i]

Children:
60,000 were victims of "substantiated or indicated" sexual abuse.[ii]

General Public:
321,500 Americans 12 and older were sexually assaulted or raped. [iii]

Military:
18,900 experienced unwanted sexual contact. [iv]

REAL SELF DEFENSE FOR WOMEN

Help for Victims

The following is information and resources that may be of interest to victims of crime. For additional information on available services in your area, visit

Office of Victims Crime's Directory of Crime Victim Services. or Office of Victims Crimes Resources for Victims Links Page

National Hotlines

Victim Services Helpline (assistance and referral)
National Center for Victims of Crime
2000 M Street NW., Suite 480
Washington, DC 20036
Phone: 1-800-FYI-CALL
TTY: 1-800-211-7996
Fax: 202-467-8701
Web site: www.ncvc.org/infolink/main.htm

The National Center for Victims of Crime's (NCVC's) mission is to help victims of crime and their families rebuild their lives. NCVC works with local, state, and federal agencies to enact legislation and provide resources, training, and technical assistance. The NCVC Web site provides relevant statistics, links to publications, and referrals to participating attorneys.

National Domestic Violence Hotline
P.O. Box 161810
Austin, TX 78716
Phone: 512-453-8117
Hotline: 1-800-799-SAFE
TTY: 1-800-787-3224
Fax: 512-453-8541
Web site: www.ndvh.org

The National Domestic Violence Hotline uses a nationwide database to provide crisis intervention, referrals, information, and support in many languages for victims of violence against women.

Rape, Abuse, and Incest National Network
635-B Pennsylvania Avenue SE.
Washington, DC 20003
Phone: 202-544-3059
Hotline: 1-800-656-HOPE
Fax: 202-544-3556
Web site: www.rainn.org

The Rape, Abuse, and Incest National Network (RAINN) offers a toll-free hotline for free, confidential counseling and support 24 hours a day for victims of rape, abuse, and incest.

National Resource Centers and Advocacy Organizations

Family Violence Prevention Fund
383 Rhode Island Street, Suite 304
San Francisco, CA 94103-5133
Phone: 415-252-8900
Fax: 415-252-8991
Web site: www.fvpf.org

The Family Violence Prevention Fund works to end domestic violence and help women and children whose lives are affected by abuse. The Web site offers free online catalogs, articles and information on abuse and violence, press releases and story archives, information on public policy efforts, and other resource materials.

Institute on Domestic Violence in the African American Community
180 McNeal Hall
University of Minnesota
1985 Buford Avenue
St. Paul, MN 55108-6142
Phone: 1-877-643-8222
Web site: www.dvinstitute.org

The Institute on Domestic Violence in the African American Community promotes public awareness through public outreach, dissemination of related information and resources, publication of a biannual newsletter, and coordination of conferences and training forums.

National Alliance of Sexual Assault Coalitions
c/o Connecticut Sexual Assault Crisis Services, Inc.
110 Connecticut Boulevard
East Hartford, CT 06108
Phone: 860-282-9881
Fax: 860-291-9335
Web site: www.connsacs.org/help/alliance.html

The National Alliance of Sexual Assault Coalitions Web site provides a listing of sexual assault coalitions across the country, with contact information, URLs, and e-mail links for each. The site includes an online library of relevant articles and information that includes research materials as well as fiction and poetry.

National Latino Alliance for the Elimination of Domestic Violence
1730 North Lynn Street, Suite 502
Arlington, VA 22209
Phone: 1-800-342-9908
Fax: 1-800-600-8931
Web site: www.dvalianza.org

The National Latino Alliance for the Elimination of Domestic Violence (the Alianza) includes Latino advocates, community activists, practitioners, researchers, and survivors of domestic violence working together to eliminate domestic violence in Latino communities. The Alianza serves as a national forum for ongoing dialogue, education, and advocacy. Publications and the Web site are offered in English and Spanish.

National Network to End Domestic Violence
666 Pennsylvania Avenue SE., Suite 303
Washington, DC 20003
Phone: 202-543-5566
Fax: 202-543-5626
Web site: www.nnedv.org

The National Network to End Domestic Violence (NNEDV) is a membership organization for state domestic violence coalitions that offers advocacy, information, referrals, technical assistance, training, and other opportunities for advocates across the country. NNEDV publishes a quarterly newsletter and the Web site includes an "On the Hill" page that tracks the latest legislation and government actions on domestic violence.

National Resource Center on Domestic Violence
Pennsylvania Coalition Against Domestic Violence
6400 Flank Drive, Suite 1300
Harrisburg, PA 17112
Phone: 1-800-537-2238
TTY: 1-800-533-2508
Fax: 717-545-9456
Web site: www.pcadv.org/projects.html

The National Resource Center on Domestic Violence (NRC) is a valuable source for information, training, and technical assistance regarding domestic violence issues. NRC is also a clearinghouse for domestic violence resources and statistics that may be used to enhance policies and publications.

National Sexual Violence Resource Center
123 North Enola Drive
Enola, PA 17025
Phone: 1-877-739-3895
TTY: 717-909-0715
Fax: 717-909-0714
Web site: www.nsvrc.org

The National Sexual Violence Resource Center (NSVRC) is a clearinghouse for resources and research about all forms of sexual violence. NSVRC works with its partner agency, the University of Pennsylvania, to provide new policies for establishing sexual violence interventions and prevention programs.

Stalking Resource Center
National Center for Victims of Crime
2000 M Street NW., Suite 480
Washington, DC 20036
Phone: 202-467-8700
Fax: 202-467-8701
Web site: www.ncvc.org/src/index.html

The National Center for Victims of Crime's (NCVC's) mission is to help victims of crime and their families rebuild their lives. The Stalking Resource Center provides resources, training, and technical assistance to criminal justice professionals and victim service providers to support locally coordinated, multidisciplinary anti-stalking approaches and responses.

In today's society, the need for real protection is neither an over sensed fear nor a false self-protective feeling of insecurity. This is a real necessity that has long been overdue. The facts and figures located in this book are not an attempt to scare or give any person a misleading characterization of crime against women. These are the real statistics from real crimes committed arbitrarily against the female gender.

None of the numbers can even come close to the actual amount of unreported crimes. The law enforcement agencies involved with the data collecting and distribution of these numbers are far from accurate as in most cases the crimes go unreported or far worse unnoticed by authorities.

In the majority of countries with available data, less than 40 percent of the women who experience violence seeks the help of any sort. Among women who do, most look to family and friends and very few look to formal institutions and mechanisms, such as police and health services. Less than 10 percent of those women seeking help for an experience of violence sought help by appealing to the police.

At least 144 countries have passed laws on domestic violence, and 154 have laws on sexual harassment. However, even when laws exist, this does not mean they are always compliant with international standards and recommendations or implemented.

Availability of data on violence against women has increased significantly in recent years. Since 1995, more than 100 countries have conducted at least one survey addressing the issue. More than 40 countries conducted at least two surveys in the period between 1995 and 2014, which means that, depending on the comparability of the surveys, changes over time could be analyzed.

The reality of today is that it is up to us to empower our own abilities to defend ourselves and keep our families from harm without the aid of others to protect us. In these tumultuous times of unrest and uneasy or unguarded situations we ourselves need to be ever more vigilant in the day to day routines we find ourselves in.

It is those times when we forget to lock the door that someone may enter. When we travel to our car with our phones attached to our ear and our attention unaware of our surroundings that we face the most eminent of threats. When we return to our homes and fumble to find our keys and are not paying attention to people walking past that we have more to fear. At these times are we most vulnerable and susceptible to an attack on our person.

How do we face these fearful events? Can we overcome an attack from behind? How will we be sure that any training we have done will actually work?

I personally have no answers to these questions. These are questions that each person must find their own answers to. Each individual is different and will react or act in a different way to any of these situations. Even a hardened trained fighter can be the victim of an unknowing attack. This being said however training and practicing can be the single element that breaks the barrier from victim to victor in a given situation.

In the material given in this manual, I hope that you are more informed and have a better sense of the realities that you may face in a face to face confrontation with any aggressor. The foundations of protection lay within your own education and study. The idea of this book was to better prepare women for an event to happen rather than shy away from the reality that it does happen to people like you every day. Without question, it is a true testimony of understanding, the need to make yourself aware of the possibilities and guard yourself against danger rather than to blindly go through life's activities with a false sense of security and unwarranted protective bubble you may feel you have against an attack.

The bubble will surely burst and the security you once felt will be replaced with the harshness of a violent attack upon your person. Losing your valuables is something you can recover from but losing one's dignity or physical damage that often comes with such aggressive behavior is something that many people can never recover from.

Ultimately you are in charge of your life, home, property security, and protection. Having the knowledge of how to handle that responsibility is now firmly on your shoulders.

That is real self-defense for women.

ABOUT THE AUTHOR

REAL SELF DEFENSE FOR WOMEN

Allen Woodman has devoted his entire life to martial arts in one form or another. 2019 marks his 46th year in the development of his martial arts and self-defense training.

After spending more than 20 years in Asia in the constant study he returned to the United States to teach martial arts and reality-based self-defense systems to the masses.

Allen has been directly involved in hand to hand instruction to the Military and Law Enforcement for many years. Training with and instructing members of the L.A.P.D., Bakersfield Sherriff's Office, S.D.P.D., Texas D.P.S., N.Y.P.D., California Highway Patrol, Las Vegas Metro Police and Agents of the F.B.I., C.I.A., and D.H.S., as well as Counter Terrorism Training Groups.

Mr. Woodman brings to the table his valuable insight and perspective of practical and useful skills. Allen is also an honorary member of the New York City Guardian Angels and his New York City School has been the headquarters for the Guardian Angels combat training for street survival.

He is currently an Instructor for C.R.I. (Counter-Terrorism training) and has been certified for Hand to Hand combat training, Women's Self Defense training, Instructor Training and is a qualified F.A.S.S.T. Tactical Communications instructor.

As a martial artist and 6th degree Black Belt in multiple martial arts, he is a World Champion Competitor, winning 3 World Titles at International Events held. Winning in multiple categories such as International Rules Self Defense, Open Self Defense and Traditional Forms competition in the senior Black Belt Division.

Allen Woodman has authored over 20 books and manuals of instruction and can be seen in many instructional videos on the common market.

Allen has trained with great instructors and gained noted rank in Philippine Arts under Grandmaster Ramiro Estalilla Jr., Punong Guro Dan Inosanto, Grandmaster Cacoy Canete, Grandmaster Ben Largusa, Grandmaster Leo Gaje, and Guro Ted LucayLucay

In traditional Japanese Arts, he has had direct training and ranking with Sosai Mas Oyama (Founder of Kyokushin Karate), Sensei R. Sato, Sensei Walter Todd, Sensei John Denora, Sensei Otto Johnson, Sensei M. Nakamura, Sensei Y. Tanaka, Shihan Joe Miller, Sensei Morio Higoanna, Sensei Fumio Demura, and Sensei M. Ueshiba.

In Chinese arts, he has exclusively trained with Sigung Ip Chun (Eldest son of Ip Man, Teacher to Bruce Lee), Sifu Samuel Kwok, Sifu Douglas Wong, and Grandmaster Eric Lee.

In Korean Arts Allen has trained exclusively with Grandmaster Won Ik Yi in the art of Tukong Moosul Won, and Tae Kwon Do under the direct tutelage of Grandmaster Jhoon Rhee.

In 1987-1988 Mr. Woodman won the honors in his Army unit as the Donnybrook Boxing Champion in consecutive years. Winning 8 of 12 fights by K.O.

Allen Woodman has been an instrumental figure and pioneer in the martial arts community for many years. Hosting and promoting the first ever martial arts convention in America between 1994-1997 as well as being the editor in chief and publisher for the semi-national SIDEKICK Martial Arts magazine from 1992-1997.

He was the driving force in supporting the first-ever trip to America for Ip Chun and Samuel Kwok in 1993 to share the art of Wing Chun Kung Fu across the United States through informative seminars and hands-on workshops.

Mr. Woodman has been inducted in over 15 Martial Arts hall of fames and Honored by the Martial Arts History Museum on 3 separate occasions in Burbank California for his contributions to the martial arts community worldwide.

Currently when schedules permit Allen works on several film and television projects as a producer, stuntman, and fight coordinator for action scenes.

He has been involved in more than 30 movies and TV shows and has starred in several action films such as Knights of Justice (1996), Running Time (1997), Street girls (1997) and smaller roles in action films such as Sworn Justice (1996), Rumble in the Bronx (1994), Night Mistress (2018) and 7 Days Alive (2018) as well as many others.

Allen has dedicated himself in his numerous books as the historian of martial arts history for the next generation. His extensive published list of books includes

- My karate a personal journey (2010)
- Introduction to American Wado Ryu (2011)
- History of Japanese Martial Arts (2012)
- Taizan Ryu Taiho Jitsu (Military Police Apprehension System) (2012)
- Hojojutsu The art of tying your enemy (2014)
- Hojojutsu The Binding Art (2016)
- The Healing Touch Complete (2019)

Allen Woodman still travels throughout the United States and around the world teaching lectures and hands on Seminars to many. From Canada to Mexico and India to Puerto Rico he can be found inspiring the next generation of martial artist.

ACCOMPANIED SELF DEFENSE CONTRIBUTER
15 X WORLD SELF-DEFENSE CHAMPION JOHN GILL

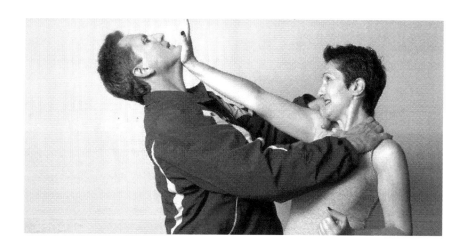

John Gill is the current world self-defense champion and winner of 26 Martial arts titles including 15 world championships won at the World Championships of Martial Arts in Las Vegas run by Grandmaster Stan Witz of the International martial Arts Council (IMAC). He has competed in the over 18 years of age Black Belt divisions since 1999. He is a 7th Dan black belt Master instructor in Hapkido and Taekwondo and won the 2016 Action Star event guaranteeing him a role in an action martial arts movie next year with Anima studios.

He was inducted into the USA Martial Arts Hall of Fame as 2016 and 2017 Hapkido Master of the Year and also inducted into the USA Martial Arts Hall of Fame as 2017 Black belt competitor of the Year.

John Gill is and is also the Australian record-holder for the most individual world title wins in Australian sporting history in any sport. He is an ambassador for the White Ribbon Foundation for the prevention of violence against women now is now assisting in promoting the International Day for the Elimination of Violence against women worldwide. He is a current and seven-time nominee for Australian of the Year for his contribution to women's and children's safety, John was named local Sportsperson of the Year at the 2013 Australia Day awards.

He has featured numerous times on national radio and television and works as a Master instructor for the Australian School of Self Defense, the Los Angeles School of Self Defense, the USA School of Self Defense and Motivational Masters. John has taught self-defense workshops in Australian schools since 1985. He has also taught at Anaheim and Orange County high schools in the USA and corporate motivational Empowerment workshops.

Master John Gill is also the Founder of the world's first comprehensive safety and Health system for Seniors called Taikido which is a non-contact and easy to learn self-defense, personal safety and health system which combines very simple techniques from Hapkido and Kung Fu for seniors to protect themselves and includes the health movements and benefits of Tai Chi. John is featured with Arnold Schwarzenegger in a current published book "Think Big" by Cydney O'Sullivan and is also featured in the 2017 'Who's who of Martial Arts'.

CONTRIBUTERS

Counter Terrorism Training School

A Special thank you to the professional staff and instructors at C.R.I. Counter Terrorism training School in Las Vegas Nevada.

Without their overwhelming help and support this book would not have been possible.

Doron Benbenisty	Founder and President
Jeremy Harris	CEO
Johnathon Alvarez	Vice President
Harrison Arager	Jr. Vice President
Katie Burlis	Krav Haganah Instructor

ABOUT CRISIS RESPONSE INTERNATIONAL
ISRAELI COUNTER TERRORISM TRAINING SCHOOL

OUR MISSION

CRI Counter Terrorism Training School offers the most comprehensive instruction to military, law enforcement, dignitary protection, private security, civilians, professional bodyguards and federal agencies in the Israeli method of training for combat and peacekeeping situations. The Israeli method of training offers a special and unique knowledge of countering terrorism, guerrilla warfare, and crime. CRI's sole purpose is to provide the most tactically realistic training as possible. We understand that, when our trainees leave our school, they may only have one chance to "get it right" in a hostile situation.

OUR VISION

Our vision is to continue to be one of the most trusted companies contributing to the security and freedom of our nation and its allies. As a counter-terrorism training leader, we will continue to develop new methods of combating modern terrorism against our nation and the world. As a vocational school, it is our goal to continue to make a positive impact on our students' lives and livelihood.

THE SCHOOL

C.R.I. Counter Terrorism Training School is a vocational school licensed to operate by the Nevada Commission on Post-secondary Education. We are also approved to accept VA Educational Benefits for a number of our courses. We have a wide variety course and many more to come. C.R.I. has been in operation since 2000 as a private instructional school, earning numerous commendations for its excellence in training.

GET IT RIGHT

The Israeli method of training offers a special and unique knowledge of countering terrorism, guerrilla warfare, and crime. C.R.I.'s sole purpose is to provide the most tactically realistic training as possible. We understand that, when our trainees leave our school, they may only have one chance to "get it right" in a hostile situation.

COMPREHENSIVE INSTRUCTION

C.R.I. combines a mixture of the reactive and the proactive approach. We do this by using advanced methods with superior instructors that enable the level of training to be as close to reality as possible. We understand that when our trainees leave the school, they may only have one chance to "get it right" in a hostile situation.

For more information please contact CRI Directly

**2421 East Gowan Rd.
North Las Vegas, Nevada 89030
Tel: 1 - 702 - 222 - 3489**

Email: **CRI@CRITRAINING.COM**

SOURCES

Matthew J. Breiding et al., Prevalence and Characteristics of Sexual Violence, Stalking, and Intimate Partner Violence Victimization - National Intimate Partner and Sexual Violence Survey, 2011, (Atlanta: CDC, 2014).

Bureau of Justice Statistics, National Crime Victimization Survey, Concatenated File, 1992-2015.

M.L. Walters et al., The National Intimate Partner and Sexual Violence Survey: 2010 Findings on Victimization by Sexual Orientation, (Atlanta: CDC, 2013).

U.S. Department of Defense, DoD Plan to Prevent and Respond to Sexual Assault of Military Men, (Arlington, VA: 2016).

Allen J. Beck et al., Sexual Victimization in Prisons and Jails Reported by Inmates, 2011-2012, (Washington, DC: Bureau of Justice Statistics, U.S. Department of Justice, 2013).

M.C. Black et al., The National Intimate Partner and Sexual Violence Survey (NISVS): 2010 Summary Report, (Atlanta: CDC, 2011).

Cora Peterson et al., "Lifetime Economic Burden of Rape Among U.S. Adults," Am J Prev Med (Jan 2017).

Christopher Krebs et al., "Campus Climate Survey Validation Study Final Technical Report," (Washington, DC: Bureau of Justice Statistics, U.S. Department of Justice, 2016), David Cantor et al., "Report on the AAU Campus Climate Survey on Sexual Assault and Sexual Misconduct," (Westat, 2017).

World Health Organization, Department of Reproductive Health and Research, London School of Hygiene and Tropical Medicine, South African Medical Research Council (2013).

Global and regional estimates of violence against women: prevalence and health effects of intimate partner violence and non-partner sexual violence.

The World's Women 2015, Trends and Statistics, Violence against Women, United Nations Department of Economic and Social Affairs, 2015 and UN Women Global Database on Violence against Women.

Promundo and UN Women (2017) *Understanding Masculinities: Results from the International Men and Gender Equality Survey – Middle East and North Africa.*

For Lebanon information, see *Understanding Masculinities: Results from the International Men and Gender Equality Survey (IMAGES) in Lebanon.*

United Nations Office on Drugs and Crime (2014).

Data for Latin America and the Caribbean was taken from the *Gender Equality Observatory for Latin America and the Caribbean* on October 2018.

UNODC (2016). Global Report on Trafficking in Persons 2016.

UNICEF (2018). *Child Marriage: Latest Trends and Future Prospects.*

UNICEF (2017). Is every child counted? Status of Data for Children in the SDGs.

UNICEF (2016). Female Genital Mutilation/Cutting: A global concern; and United Nations (2018). *Intensifying Global Efforts for the Elimination of Female Genital Mutilation, Report of the Secretary-General.*

UNICEF (2017). *A Familiar Face: Violence in the lives of children and adolescents.*

UNESCO (2018). *School violence and bullying: Global status and trends, drivers and consequences.*

Education for All Global Monitoring Report (EFA GMR), UNESCO, United Nations Girls' Education Initiative (UNGEI) (2015).

School-related gender-based violence is preventing the achievement of quality education for all, Policy Paper 17UNGEI (2014).

Federal Bureau of Investigation (2017) Violent crime report/

James Comey F.B.I. Director Statement of crime report (2016)

Cantor, D., Fisher, B., Chibnall, S., Townsend, R., Lee, H., Bruce, C., and Thomas, G. (2015).

Report on the AAU Campus Climate Survey on Sexual Assault and Sexual Misconduct.

John Gill Defensive Arts Instructor Melbourne, Sydney, Australia. (2019)

European Union Agency for Fundamental Rights (2014). *Violence against women: an EU-wide survey.*

Promundo and UN Women (2017) *Understanding Masculinities: Results from the International Men and Gender Equality Survey – Middle East and North Africa.*

Australian Human Rights Commission (2018).

Bakersfield California U.S.A. Sheriff's Office Intercity Crime report (2015)

Everyone's business: Fourth National Survey on Sexual Harassment in Australian Workplaces. Inter-Parliamentary Union (2016).

United Nations Economic and Social Affairs (2015). The World's Women 2015, Trends and Statistics.

World Bank Group (2018). *Women, Business and the Law 2018*, database.

United Nations Economic and Social Affairs (2015). The World's Women 2015, Trends and Statistics.

European Union Agency for Fundamental Rights (2014). Violence against women: an EU-wide survey, Annex 3,

Australian Human Rights Commission (2017). *Change the Course: National Report on Sexual Assault and Sexual Harassment at Australian Universities.*

Dunkle K., Van Der Heijden I., Stern E., and Chirwa E. (2018). *Disability and Violence against Women and Girls: Emerging Evidence from the What Works to Prevent Violence against Women and Girls Global Programme,*

Devries, K., Kyegome, N., Zuurmond, M., Parkes, J., Child, J., Walakira, E. and Naker, D. (2014). Violence against primary school children with disabilities in Uganda: a cross-sectional study.

CDC (2016). *Youth Risk Behavior Surveillance—United States, 2015.*

Los Angeles Police Department Crime Statistics and report (2016).
Las Vegas Metropolitan Police Department and Enforcement Crime Statistics (2017).

Australian Human Rights Commission (2018). *Everyone's business: Fourth National Survey on Sexual Harassment in Australian Workplaces.*

C.R.I. Counter Terrorism Training School / Urban Warrior program Las Vegas, Nevada, U.S.A. (2019)

Allen Woodman Womens Self Defense Instruction Las Vegas Nevada, U.S.A. (2019)

New York Times Newspaper (2018)

Los Angela's Times Newspaper (2018)

United States Library of Congress (2018)

Time Magazine (2018)

UMAATC Hot line Information (2019)

Goldie Mack (2019

Made in the USA
Monee, IL
25 February 2024

53572603R00162